COSMIC LOVE SIGNS

The Astrological
Way to Meet Men

COSMIC
LOVE
SIGNS

by JOANNE
LEMIEUX

Prentice Hall Press · New York

Published by Prentice Hall Press
A Division of Simon & Schuster, Inc.
Gulf + Western Building
One Gulf + Western Plaza
New York, NY 10023

PRENTICE HALL PRESS is a trademark of Simon & Schuster, Inc.

Library of Congress Cataloging in Publication Data

Lemieux, Joanne, 1946–
    Cosmic love signs.

    1. Astrology. 2. Love—Miscellanea. I. Title.
BF1729.L6L44   1986   133.5'864677   85-30079
ISBN 0-668-06588-5

Manufactured in the United States of America

10 9 8 7 6 5 4 3 2 1

First Edition

Dedicated to my Grandmother,
Anna Elizabeth Pukallus Hero

Acknowledgments

For every season under the stars, there is a purpose, and for those who plant in that season, they will reap the rewards of their harvest.

All my love to my daughter, Suzanne, and my husband, Richard.

A special thank you to my assistant, Margaret Clandon-Cousins, my graphic designer, Bonnie Uttech, and my agent, Susan Harris, who have been with me from the very beginning.

My sincerest appreciation to Donna Bellinger, Helen Gallegos, and Dorothy Vitter, who so generously gave of their time, and to all the other people who actively participated in this research.

And to Madelyn Larsen, who made this whole book possible. Again, to everyone—thank you.

Contents

Introduction

This book is about love and love signs; it is a how-to book that will put more romance back into your life. *How to* get it, *how to* keep it, and *how to* continually have an aura of romance surrounding you, even if you don't have a man on your arm—this takes know-how and the resolve to be yourself and no one else.

Romance . . . love . . . woman . . . man . . . part . . . counterpart. That is a woman's function in life: to attract the male of the species and continue our race. As long as there are human beings, the two sexes will always complement each other.

Like most women, I want to be beautiful, glamorous, and, if not alluring, at least attractive. Why is it that the majority of us want the same thing? Why is it that we spend days, weeks, even months, in dieting and deprivation? So that we might be able to fit into that perfect size ten dress? Every year women spend thousands of dollars and hundreds of hours trying to find just the right product or technique that promises a winning edge on the competition, or at least one-upmanship on the girl next door. Women feel that they must compete for attention and be attractive to members of the opposite sex. When we are noticed and courted by men, our confidence soars. We are popular, we are accepted, we belong. But let us be ignored and we descend into the jaws of hell, lamenting the cruel fate that has made us unattractive and unacceptable to our counterpart.

Some women naturally know how to attract. Their timing, elegance, and grace are impeccable. But women like you and me have to learn to practice our technique. By learning how to capitalize on our given talents and our individual timing (as foretold by our horoscope), we learn how to take advantage of our astrological transits. We no longer simply get older—we have to get better.

First, you must learn about yourself and where and when you can shine. Remember, a diamond in the rough is not a pretty sight. Many of us would pass one by, even if it were in our own backyard, because we do not know what to look for. Once the diamond is cut and polished, its sparkle can affect the coldest heart. You are a diamond in the rough. Now it is time for you to be cut and polished to a warm glow, to bring out your sparkling brilliance.

Each of us has her own style, her own grace, her own body language, her own allure, and her own beauty. The problem is, the majority of us have not learned to use what we have to our best advantage. For one reason or another, we may not realize we have "it," and instead have camouflaged our true identity by imitating someone else whose style does not lend itself well to our person. This, in turn, gives others a conflicting and confusing message.

Society has dealt many women a low blow by making youth and beauty its symbols. The models we use to measure and compare ourselves with usually are under thirty years of age, are tall, and weigh around a hundred pounds. Personally, I'm waiting for Rubens' women to come back into vogue, but I have a feeling I will have a long wait! Thank God, there are still some men out there who appreciate a well-rounded woman. In the meantime, I will continue to give up potato chips, eat salads for lunch, and faithfully pass up desserts—well, almost faithfully!

Where is all this leading? Down the right path, I hope. You *can* have it all without changing the real you. How? With astrology. By allowing your natural timing, your givens, and your environment to conform to you and your needs, you can have the man of your dreams.

The purpose of this book is to explain how, where, and when—through astrology—to find, attract, and keep the kind of man you are seeking. The best way to do this is by accentuating the positive and eliminating the negative. Sound easy? It isn't. Very few of us can be objective about ourselves or our flaws. We tend to magnify our faults and work only on them, to the exclusion of our good points. Determine what is right about you and concentrate on making your good points even better. To do this, first read the chapter on your sun sign; then take a piece of paper and write down fifty things about yourself that are special. From this list, pick ten things that you like and resolve to make them better. For example, If you have a nice bustline, experiment with pretty undergarments that will give you a shapely silhouette and are a flattering style, color, and fit. Or if you have beautiful eyes, experiment with eye makeup to give yourself a new, different, exciting look that can be changed from day to day. You get the picture.

If you learn nothing else from this book, learn how to smile. A smile is universal and says, "Hi, I like you and would like to know you better." When you smile, mean it. People don't always show it, but everyone responds to a smile.

Most of the men who helped contribute to this book remarked that what first attracted them to a woman was "She smiled at me." Think back—remember the times you were in a room full of strangers and how unbearable it was until someone smiled at you and acknowledged that you were there? You felt you had an ally. That made you feel better, and you can make someone else feel good by smiling.

Before we get to the good part—yourself—we must first look at the man who is out there, waiting to discover you.

ARIES The first men to discover are the Aries natives. These men are fast and racy, love sports, fast cars, and sexy women, and are usually very good-looking. They live on a tightrope and love competition. These men can be expected to compete for everything—jobs, women, even the dinner tab. If you like a macho man, an Aries man is for you.

What is this attractive Aries man looking for in a lady? Just that—a lady, in every sense of the word. He won't mind a little competition to keep the game interesting, but remember—he likes to think he has won the prize, because he likes to win. Aries men like the idea of having a lady that other men covet, and looks are very important to them. You will always have to look your best, because you will be on display. Smile. He is awfully proud of you.

⊖

TAURUS The bull. This man will remind you of a bull. Nothing weak-looking about him. Beneath that teddy bear exterior beats the heart of a true connoisseur. Taurus natives know how to treat a lady. Fine wine, good food, and best of all, this man is a member of the money signs. He can always be counted on to find money for you to spend. The Taurus man is very set in his ways and doesn't like surprises. Please don't try to play complicated head games, because he is no game player. He means what he says—and you'd better pay attention.

What kind of woman is this man looking for? If you are rich, you are definitely in the running, but if not, you still have a good chance. Taurus men can go to extremes when it comes to women. He will either gravitate to the very practical, earth mother type or to the very exotic. Remember: no games! This man's heart is very fragile, and he really is a dear.

♊

GEMINI Dashing is the only way to describe this native. Dashing here, there, and everywhere, all at the same time and usually in different directions. You may need track shoes to keep up with this one! He will slow down only long enough to flash you the brightest smile you have ever seen. Maybe he will chitchat a bit, displaying not only his superior intellect and wit but also his genuine interest in you. If you like a fun, popular guy, then this one may interest you, but be prepared to share him with the world. His curiosity and interests are many and never-ending. Geminis really hate to be weighed down by the practical side of life. The Gemini native likes his women to be as intellectually stimulating as he is, and he likes a woman who loves to master new games. This man is not a male chauvinist; he is looking for an equal, a partner. His advertisement for the perfect woman would read:

> WANTED: Healthy, sexy, outdoorsy, artistic woman, with a
>   free spirit.
> Object: Chance to play some new, fascinating, interesting games.

♋

CANCER Our moon man is just that—a man who appears to change with the phases of the moon. This man literally has stars in his eyes, and his moods seem to change right in front of your eyes. His highs are the highest and his lows the lowest, but in reality the Cancer man never really changes. His heart is always constant. He is the most loyal, dearest, kindest, and gentlest man in the zodiac. If he gives you his love, there is nothing he won't do for you. This man has a habit of doing for others. Be kind to him. He will blossom under love's eternal light, and the chances that he might become a millionaire are much higher than those of any other sign of the zodiac. Cancer natives are drawn to anyone who will love them for themselves. They can bring out the passion as well as the maternal instinct in any woman. This man won't mind if you want to head your own corporation; he will not only encourage you, he may also help finance it.

♌

LEO The lion, king of the jungle. Perhaps the hardest male to attract, catch, and keep. Everyone loves a lover, and this one loves everyone!

He can be found on bright, sunny days worshipping the sun or on cool, summer evenings delighting others with his wit and antics. Leo men appear to do for everyone but themselves. They just don't have time to waste, are in great demand, and love attention. Leo seeks his own kind and loves to play rescuer. He wants someone who is unusual, loves change, and has a fire that burns as brightly as his own. To attract this man's attention, wear unusual clothes, something unique and very dramatic and eye-catching. Remember, if you aren't the type to carry it off, this man will know, and he will be very disappointed when he finds out that you aren't what you appear to be—because he is. No phonies need apply.

♍

VIRGO These men hate to be boring. They will go to great lengths to be funny and witty, and they really do have a great sense of humor. They can usually be found in banks, counting out their money. They are rather frugal, but when they buy something they buy the very best. Virgo natives stay on top of everything, love organization, and will reach high positions of prominence and responsibility through hard work and perseverance. These men can be quite self-critical and really need a pat on the back, a few kind words, and lots of TLC. They gravitate to the woman who can make their dreams come true; they work hard and don't complain. Their needs are simple. They are affected by wanderlust, and once in a while they need to get a glimpse of the world through rose-colored glasses. With this, they can create a more beautiful world for you and for themselves. A kindhearted woman will do nicely. For love, they will lovingly share everything they own. Virgo men really care—treasure them.

LIBRA This man is looking for the perfect woman, a woman he can be proud of. Libran men love to show you off, because they think you are something special. The woman this man chooses has to have an active interest in the world at large and be exceptionally pretty or attractive. He also likes someone who thinks as much of herself as he does. If you have low self-esteem or a poor self-image you will turn him off, because he will start to wonder what he ever saw in you. Don't fish for compliments from this one; he will give them willingly and often.

♏

SCORPIO These men have a reputation for being passionate. They are—both in and out of bed—but they don't really like to talk about it. In fact, Scorpios rarely tell everything they know until they feel they can trust you. Scorpio men have always enjoyed a dark reputation. Haven't you found that Scorpio men are somehow fascinating, if not downright hypnotic and ever so intriguing? What hidden traits is this man secretly searching for? Above all else, he wants someone he can trust. Someone who can help him obtain all his hidden desires and dreams. He will demand total loyalty and honesty, and he will love you with his whole being, as you have never been loved before. It gives me goose bumps just thinking about him! If you can't match his passion, don't get into his fire, because you will definitely get burned.

♐

SAGITTARIUS If I were going to a party, the Sag man is the one I would like on my arm. Sag men are usually handsome, in a rugged sort of way, and have a dog or horse tucked away. Their philosophy is "Love me, love my dog." They believe animals have the good sense to judge a person's true motives, even if they can't. So be prepared to love animals, the outdoors, sports, and having a good time. A Sag man is lots of fun, but he does demand his freedom, and in return he will grant you yours. The Sagittarian man will look for the lady who has the confidence and guts to be herself. He really admires that in a woman. He hates to be tied down and would never do that to you, but he does like games, adventure, and anyone who is in perpetual motion. Even as he grows older, he will always remain active and virile. If you want to pique his interest, wear the color blue and don't slow down! Don't worry—he will catch up with you sooner than you think.

♑

CAPRICORN This is my favorite sign. See that serious man over there in the corner, talking business with an associate or two? This man misses nothing, but it may be a little harder to get this type to admit that he is attracted to you. You see, he is very cautious. He wants to be very sure he won't be humiliated or rejected, and he is rather shy, so be gentle. Capricorn won't mind if you want to make the first move, so long as it is ladylike. Once assured that his advances won't be rejected, he will come after you with marriage on his mind; he doesn't like to mess around. Capricorn men like to be married. He wants a girl just like the girl that married dear old dad. And he usually finds her. He will not mind if you work or do your own thing. In fact, he will be proud of you in an understated way, but you had best have dinner on the table and love children, because he loves playing father to you and he won't even mind playing father to your little girl. All you have to remember is that he takes everything seriously.

AQUARIUS Gregarious, these men make the most delightful playmate, friend, companion, and cohort in intrigue. No woman can resist an Aquarian on the prowl—you can't help falling in love with him. Even if it doesn't work out, this man will want to remain your friend and will continue to call, just to see how you are doing or to raise your spirits if you are feeling low. Keep this one around even if you aren't serious, because he will be a good, loyal friend and will always be there when you need him. What type of woman is he attracted to? A dynamic, dramatic one. One who gets things done and does it with flair and panache. You must also like people. Aquarians have never been known to be cheapskates, so don't you be, or he will be turned off completely. For him, half the fun is the show, the splash. Remember, he is looking for a friend first and a lover second.

PISCES A delightful sign. I have never known a Piscean man I didn't like! These men go through life with rose-colored glasses. If you are lucky enough to land this one, he will never see the gray hairs, the wrinkles, or the extra few pounds you might add over the years. He will always see you as the lovely girl he fell in love with. It is hard to say who catches this man's attention, because he doesn't seem to walk with both feet on the ground. He usually has his head in the clouds and his heart on his sleeve. Opposites do attract. The Pisces man usually ends up with the practical woman, who can help turn his dreams into reality. This type of relationship works out well because both partners respect each other's talents. Be kind to a Piscean man and he can overlook any other faults you may have.

Now that you know something about the different men of the zodiac and what they are like, how do you pick the right one? Should you look for a particular sign? The answer is that each sign has its good points and its less good points. There will be certain signs that you will just naturally attract and will immediately identify with. You will find you are just more comfortable with men of your own element—fire: Aries, Leo, and Sagittarius; earth: Taurus, Virgo, and Capricorn; air: Gemini, Libra, and Aquarius; and water: Cancer, Scorpio, and Pisces.

It is best to remember that each man is an individual; he possesses the potential for a meaningful, loving relationship until or unless he proves otherwise.

 *Aries*

Aries women tend to relate much better to men than to other women. Mars, your ruling planet, seems to have given you an advantage over the rest of your sisters, and you instinctively know how to use it. You appear to understand men more easily, and they appear to understand you. You may not know when to use this ability, but in most cases you certainly seem to use it at the right time.

Do you love expensive clothes? Extravagant presents? Do you have to be the first in your condo to try the latest fad or the newest diet? Can you create a whole new look without even thinking about it, until someone comments on how terrific you look? Then you are a typical, not-so-typical Aries. The most important things in life for you are that you are different and the best that you can be. It is lucky for you that you occupy the first sign in the zodiac, which gives you the confidence to carry it off.

Aries is the first, cardinal fire sign. Your symbol is the victorious ram. Characterized, you are pictured as a knight in shining armor, riding a fiery steed, charging in where angels fear to tread, trying to right a wrong to protect the innocent. Joan of Arc most certainly personifies the Aries characteristics. No true Aries can tolerate an injustice, and she will make herself the focal point for others to rally around. Aries women never really grow old—another advantage over their sisters. You stay young by always keeping yourself open and willing to try something new or different. Your innocence and curiosity will always keep your outlook on life fresh, new, exciting, and young. You will always plunge headfirst into things, which makes life with you more exciting than with other signs. Life is fun and there is never a dull moment with you. Eloise, an Aries writer of the first order, is just such a delight. She has written everything from *The Winter War 1939–1940,* for which she received the Order of the White Rose from the Finnish government, to a new, suspenseful romantic novel that explores a woman's hidden fantasies about life, love, and the pursuit of happiness.

Somehow, Aries women always seem to get their own way. How do you do it? What is your secret? Possibly all your risk taking gives you the edge. You certainly have charisma and the confidence to bring it off. Mars has seen fit to give you an abundance of energy to draw on, which we hope you will not abuse. Take a look at Diana Ross and Bette Davis, both of whom could be role models for you. In matters of love and sex, Mars has given you a fiery appetite. Therefore, when you do choose a mate (and it is you who does the choosing), make sure it is someone who can meet your expectations. He must give you the loyalty and adoration that you never tire of and that you deserve. But he had better not be a wimp, because you need someone you can respect and look up to.

You do have a reputation for being an outrageous flirt who bores easily. Bore easily—yes. Flirt—yes. But find a man who will support you, can match your stamina, is as creative as you, likes to spend money on you, loves surprises, adores you, and is a bit of a challenge—then and only then, beware! You can be easily seduced and love every minute of it. He will be totally yours. If he ever leaves you, just keep this one thought in mind: he will never in his entire life forget you. You are that kind of woman.

Originality, anything new, flashy, or on the racy side, holds a great deal of fascination for you. A new red sports car can invade your dreams at night. If that is what you want, somehow you manage to get it. Nothing is impossible for you, because magic, fairy tales, and miracles are real to you. You make them come alive and you make them happen. That optimistic aura of yours will carry you through some of your roughest times, and somehow you will always manage to grab the brass rings in life.

Aries women are usually the pursuer and the man the pursuee. First you size a man up, then you go after him. Trouble can arise because your timing can sometimes be off. There are times when finding a man who appeals to you is very difficult, to say the least. Perhaps you are not looking in the right places or on the right day. Next time, look on a Tuesday.

Where, you may ask, are the right places? How do I use what I have? When is the best time to look? First, I will answer by saying, it all depends on the type of relationship you are looking for. Be honest with yourself.

Love, romance, and excitement can be found when you cast a casual glance around on your next vacation. You will look great and you will know it. Go to one of the resorts that cater to the sun worshippers. Or if resorts don't agree with your pocketbook, join an auto rally, take in a car race, or see an auto show. You always did have something for fast, racy cars and even faster men, and what better place to shop for that little extra something?

Looking for something more permanent, or at least more conservative? Try taking classes in art or art appreciation—pick a subject you would really like to learn about. A college course in the fall, one that attracts more men than women, should do the trick. But remember: do it for yourself first, for fun second, and for men third.

There is always bodybuilding. Whether as a spectator or a participant, Aries always did love to get physical!

I have given you some ideas about where to look, but be careful. Many Aries women are overeager. Most men like directness in a woman but shy away from sheer aggression. There is nothing wrong with being assertive; the danger lies in the type of men you will attract. As you grow older, you may attract weaker men. After that first thrill of discovery, you may become bored and disillusioned. What you want and need is a man who is your equal. Some astrologers say you may even want to be dominated. I don't believe this. You appear to be looking for a man as strong as you, a man who really cares, someone who is good in bed and creative enough to invent new ways to keep your interest.

You look best in the bright light of sunshine, when you wear colorful, fashionable clothes. You, unlike many of your sister signs, have no trouble at all gaining or attracting attention. And that is the first step toward enticement.

We have taken care of the first important step. You already know how to attract attention. If you are not sure, start by wearing something red. Some reds will look better on you than others, so I would suggest that you find your shade of red. A great book to read is Carole Jackson's *Color Me Beautiful.* It will help any woman look her best, accentuate the positive, and help her find her color palette. Use your red as one of your basic colors. You will also find that it brings you luck.

Most men love the color red on a woman because it has such drawing power. A lot of men who wouldn't ordinarily go up to a woman will find you more approachable. They will come up to you just to tell you that they love what you are wearing. (A great opening line if ever I heard one!) That is what you want: to be singled out in a crowd as someone special.

Your clothes also play an important part in attracting attention. You want to strive for that "rich witch" look—the sort of unique look Aries is famous for. You know just how to pull together an outfit. Make the best possible use of this gift. If you try to dress like someone else, it will not bring the desired results. Always trust your creative intuition. Never try to be something you are not, because you just can't pull it off.

Never surround yourself with dull colors. They aren't for you. But your clothes are just as important as your colors. You need rich-looking, well-fitting clothes that can go anyplace at a moment's notice. Try to stay away from the oversized, sloppy look. This may be good for some, but not for you.

A layered look is great and can give you versatility, but most important, you must develop your own style. Then you can be the fashion leader you were meant to be. Decide what statement you want your clothes to make. No tight clothes, however; you are an active Aries woman who needs clothes that move with you.

After appealing to his sense of sight, you must now appeal to his sense of smell. Evoke memories of the freshness of springtime. Remind him of the long, warm spring days of his youth, when his fancy turned to love. Any of the flowery fragrances should do the trick. Some examples of perfumes for Aries are Chanel No. 19, Givenchy III, and Orange Blossom. It is likely that you will find your own scent and it will be something brand-new.

Where would any woman be without jewelry? Iron and steel are your metals. Not the prettiest of metals, but the most durable. A glint of steel sets a man's heart pounding—just like an Aries woman. The gem for Aries is the diamond. This should more than make up for the "heavy metal" look. If I were to suggest a piece of jewelry to invest in, it would be earrings. Nothing less than 14 karat, of course. By wearing gold, you attract love, fun, romance, and attention to your face. With the extra, added sparkle on your ears, his eyes will be forced to focus on your face and will naturally travel across it a few times, just to take it all in. So take advantage of this kind of jewelry to capture his interest.

Good health is very important to an Aries native. In order to look and feel your best, exercise, watch what you eat, and try to relax more. Aries natives may find relaxing the hardest part of all.

Your dietary needs are few: lots of fiber from whole grains, fresh fruits and vegetables, and plenty of lean red meat. Always check to be sure everything is fresh. Never overeat when angry or upset, because this could lead to physical problems. If you feel you need to lose a few pounds, start dieting in spring, right after the full moon. You are one of the lucky ones—because you are a fire sign, you do not really need to diet. All you have to do is exercise to control your trouble spots, which are your hips and thighs.

You have great physical reflexes, or so I have been told by your Leo and Sagittarius friends. You need lots of sun and fun. Choose a recreational sport that concentrates on your great footwork. Join a tennis or racquetball club. You will find lots of action and lots of partners who are looking for a few sets during lunch or after work. After a game, treat yourself to a massage. Relieve all the tension that builds up during the day, and don't be afraid to ask about that gorgeous man you met. Your masseuse can be a wealth of information.

Most women would kill for your facial structure, which makeup artists love to work with because it is so naturally beautiful. Many a time you don't put on makeup or create a routine. You are in too much of a hurry. Begin making time. Men can't usually tell when a woman is wearing makeup, but they certainly can when she is not. Makeup covers a multitude of sins, takes years off your face, and, used correctly, enhances any woman's appearance.

A reputable makeup artist can make a few suggestions for your busy lifestyle that can make you more exciting. One word of caution: be careful what you put on your face, as Aries can be prone to breakouts. Remember, dry skin can develop as you get older. Make sure your makeup corresponds to your skin type and complements your coloring.

Aries rules the head and face; make this part of your body your focal point. I have already suggested that you wear earrings. I will now suggest a good haircut, something that is easy to take care of, with lots of potential for change, depending on your whims.

You now know where and how to use your astrological keys, and the last key will open the door to everything you need to know to attract the best things in life.

I asked before what type of relationship you really want with a man. We want different kinds of relationships at different times in our lives, and we must realize that no man can meet all of our needs. So think about the most important need you have. Are you looking for a nurturer, a lover, a partner, a financial supporter, an authority figure, or a friend?

The summer months (July 21–August 20) can be exciting if you are looking for fun and games and if you want romance. Just because you think it is love, however, don't depend on it to last. If it does, then as the sun enters Libra (September 21–October 20) the decision to make it more permanent will be addressed by both of you.

Once summer comes to a close, the first days of fall (September 21–October 20) find you at the center of many social activities. Be sure to always look your best this month, because there are a number of potential relationships coming into your orb. Do not sit at home; make yourself available, because the opportunity of a lifetime is just outside your door. Are you going to open it? The relationships you form now are of the more lasting kind.

Fall is the time of year when you will not only mingle with beautiful people, you will become one of them. Lucky you. If a special man comes along and if the feeling is mutual, this could be the match of the century. Remember, you will have many men to choose from.

As the sun enters Sagittarius (November 21–December 20) your mind may wander to foreign places, or you may be caught up in a foreign affair. There are people and places that can be very lucky for an Aries woman. These places are Puerto Rico, Denmark, and Germany, and the local people will generally bring you immediate luck. If you want to travel, language classes are an excellent investment. Learning a new language can be time consuming, so perhaps you would rather investigate England or Canada. If not, you can always ask, "Does anyone speak English?"

When the Christmas holiday spirit has left and the sun enters Aquarius (January 21–February 20), a special present is still waiting to be unwrapped by our Aries native. The best present of all, the present of friendship. The friends you make this month are special. They will be loyal, kind, and understanding. Passion and sex are wonderful, but friendships burn brighter, with a light that can last through the years. Friendships grow and remain an experience that can be shared, no matter what our age. Male friends are the best. When you are looking for answers to the complex questions involving the opposite sex, a man's point of view is invaluable. You can call him up on a dateless Saturday night and be assured (if he doesn't have a date) that he will take you out for pizza and beer and not spread it around that you are a wallflower. You can share secrets with him that you could never tell a lover, won't tell your mother, and shouldn't tell your girlfriends. All in all, a good time to look for male companionship with that little extra something called friendship.

This is your life, so go for it!

YOUR COSMIC STAR

Below is a list of the different areas of personal concern and the significance that each plays in your life. How each corresponds to your own personalized Cosmic Star is explained. When the sun passes over each area in turn, that area of your life is highlighted for approximately one month. Knowing this can be very helpful to you when you want to make an important move. This is very valuable information to have when you need to coordinate your best timing with decisive action or start a new project. You know that your cosmic year can easily be individualized. It begins with this year's birthday and ends with your next birthday.

By familiarizing yourself with each astrological area of your Cosmic Star, you will know what part of your life will be paramount and how best to take advantage of your positive qualities.

1.　♈　YOURSELF When the sun highlights Area 1, it accents your need to look and be at your best.

2. ♉ MATERIAL POSSESSIONS When the sun highlights Area 2, you become much more aware of your worth.

3. ♊ ABILITY TO COMMUNICATE When the sun highlights Area 3, you wish to exchange ideas with other people.

4. ♋ HOME AND FAMILY When the sun highlights Area 4, you would like to spend more time at home with your family.

5. ♌ LOVE LIFE When the sun highlights Area 5, what you would really like to do is just enjoy life.

6. ♍ WORK When the sun highlights Area 6, you must work hard for the things you want.

7. ♎ MARRIAGE When the sun highlights Area 7, other people could be ready to make a commitment.

8. ♏ SUPPORT When the sun highlights Area 8, you may need help.

9. ♐ TRAVEL When the sun highlights Area 9, you find good luck on the road.

10. ♑ CAREER When the sun highlights Area 10, career moves can now go public.

11. ♒ FRIENDS When the sun highlights Area 11, you meet new people and make new friends.

12. ♓ THE END When the sun highlights Area 12, everything becomes known.

HOW TO USE YOUR COSMIC STAR

The easy-to-use Cosmic Star will help you to personalize your own chart by using your birthday as a starting point. I will begin by showing you where and how your cosmic year begins.

The points of the star move in a counterclockwise direction. Each point represents approximately one month. To make it personally yours, place your birthday at the point marked 1 ♈. Then, moving down again in a counterclockwise direction, place the next month and your birthday at point 2 ♉, and so forth, placing the same day and the next month at each point until all the points are captioned.

As the year moves along, you can visualize how the sun's transits over these points each month will affect your life. You are now in a better position to

anticipate major changes and capitalize on any new opportunities that could present themselves.

If you were born at the end of one sign or at the beginning of another, then turn to Appendix A on page 115 to find out exactly what constellation the sun was moving through at the time of your birth. To check how I individualized my own Cosmic Star, turn to Appendix B on page 125.

Aries

March 21 – April 20

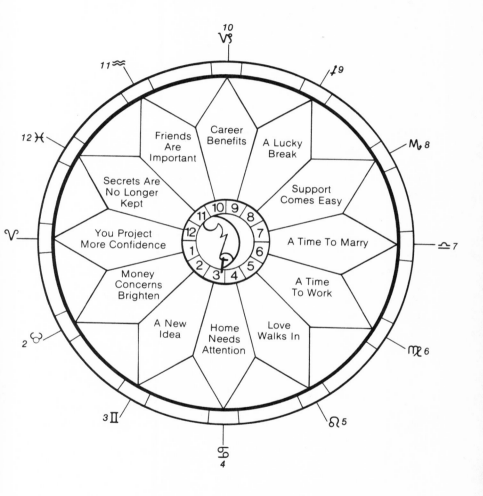

10 ♑

11 ♒

♐ 9

12 ♓

♏ 8

♈

♎ 7

2 ♉

♍ 6

3 ♊

♌ 5

♋ 4

Friends Are Important

Career Benefits

A Lucky Break

Secrets Are No Longer Kept

Support Comes Easy

You Project More Confidence

A Time To Marry

Money Concerns Brighten

A Time To Work

A New Idea

Home Needs Attention

Love Walks In

11 10 9 8 7 6 5 4 3 2 1 12

2

Taurus

The Taurus woman is definitely a springtime lady. Sunshine and luck will follow wherever you go. There is a sensuousness about you that attracts men like bees to honey. You probably feel that you really don't need to know how to attract attention because you have never lacked for male attention or male companionship. You are right! You really don't need to know because it comes so naturally to you. Perhaps what other people see in you is your natural self-assuredness. You instill in others instant confidence in you and your abilities, which puts people at ease immediately and makes them feel more comfortable around you.

A man who will best fit into your lifestyle is a man with a lot of power and just as much money. You ask for and demand the best. It's not that you are a snob, but you are very discriminating. Venus, the ruler of the astrological sign Taurus, gave you a liking for the finer things in life, and usually the finer things in life are expensive. And you, my dear Taurus, are worth every penny of it. The Taurus native loves luxury, and you usually surround yourself with all the little creature comforts you can afford. You just absolutely adore it when others surprise you with gifts that add to that comfort. You can become a little disappointed and a wee bit grumpy if a man does not show his appreciation for your company by showing you a good time. The last noteworthy item is that your man should be as good a lover as you are.

Taurus is one of the money signs of the zodiac. Lucky you. You were born to have a "silver spoon" in your mouth. You show a wonderful appreciation for the nicer things in life: crystal, fine china, sterling silver, caviar, champagne, and the more expensive designer clothes. All Taurus natives love life and all of its pleasures. Isn't it nice to know that you will never have to go totally without? You always somehow manage to find the money for those little necessities that you want. If you really want something, the money will come to you.

Knowing what your body style is can come in handy when you are deciding on a look to knock out your competition. You can go with a very feminine style like Ann-Margret, or a much more sophisticated, feminine look like Audrey Hepburn, or a much more stylish, feminine look like Cher or Barbra Streisand. No matter which look you choose, the key word is *feminine*. The real secret to being feminine is your high self-esteem and your total enjoyment of being a woman. Now isn't that simple?

If you have been experiencing a time of doubt lately, in order to achieve an even higher sense of self-esteem you should arrange to surround yourself with things that make you feel good. Many of your earth sisters like to surround themselves with all natural things, such as plants, original works of art, unusual handicrafts, natural fibers, and gifts from adoring friends, which they display with a great deal of pleasure. Why? Because it reminds them of how much they are loved and appreciated. We all want to be loved and appreciated, even when we are the gift givers.

Clothes are rather important to you and are something you naturally know a lot about. You have an eye for the very finest quality and the luck to get it at a bargain price. You should have at least one cashmere sweater set and a silk dress in your wardrobe. Textures and the actual feel of the material should be just as important as the style of the clothes. Your sense of touch is very highly developed and your skin can be very sensitive. When you try on a new piece of clothing, close your eyes and let your sense of touch tell you if this is something you will be comfortable in. Not only should it look good and feel good, it also should wear well, because you hate to throw anything out, especially an old favorite. Your clothes should be rather simple, ultrafeminine, romantic, and very elegant. They should give the illusion of a clean-cut, clearly defined line. Use lots of separates, and be sure to include at least one flowery print for spring and summer wear and one velvet suit or dress for the fall-winter festivities that you are sure to be invited to. Again, be sure all fabrics are more than 50 percent natural fiber, because of the comfort factor. Show off your shoulders whenever possible, since they are one of your best features. What turns men on physically, researchers say, are bare shoulders. Men find the look very provocative.

Clothes are important, but color has the greatest potential for drawing people and things into your orb. There is a new field devoted solely to the study of color and its effect on the individual. Pastels and the crisp, light, bright color palettes are the most effective—pink in particular. Remember the old saying "Pink is for little girls?" Well, there is much truth in that. Men love pink on women. Research shows that pink marks people who are accessible or approachable. Pink is one of the most submissive colors on the color wheel. The red draws men in and the brightness of the hue holds them spellbound.

Certain types of accessories are needed to complete the look. Jade or coral will bring you luck. Always be sure to wear a simple but very elegant necklace or pendant. Use it to draw attention to your beautiful neck and, again, show off your pretty bare shoulders. Most important, don't *ever* wear cheap jewelry. Never wear an old piece of jade unless you know where it has been and who has worn it before. An old Oriental belief says that jade is reputed to hold the vibrations of its previous wearers, and if they were unhappy, "so shall ye be."

Makeup is fun to use and experiment with. It can also be used to enhance any face. But no matter what I tell you, you are going to use the same regime you have always used, because you are comfortable with it. If you are showing any signs of sensitivity to the products you have been using, find something more compatible with your skin type and seek professional help to update your look. Today, many cosmetic counters in the finer department stores have trained their personnel in the use of their products and the latest makeup techniques. Many of them are willing to teach you what they have learned, at no extra expense to you.

It's getting late; you are almost ready to leave. The last thing you do before you leave the house is dab a little bit of perfume behind each ear and at the base of your neck. If you have been buying cologne or perfume in the large bottles, be careful. Once you open it, chemical changes start taking place and a fragrance can change. Also, after a while it may even react differently to your body chemistry, creating another change in scent. Buy a small bottle instead. When choosing a scent for yourself, find an earthy fragrance that gives you just a whisper of spice, such as Je Reviens, Halston, or Norell. Now off you go!

As I mentioned in the beginning, you are a springtime gal who should always surround yourself with the trappings of a spring day. What do you think of when you think of spring? Green plants, picnics, flowers, natural daylight (or as close to natural light as you can get), and being outdoors. If you can't manage to get outdoors, then bring spring into your home.

Love and having fun come easily between August 21 and September 20. It's a great time to go on vacation and just to plain enjoy yourself, but you already know how to do that. You are the marrying kind, but even though love is here and you think it can go on forever, it is only fun and games and not necessarily a long-lasting relationship. Choose your partners carefully. A relationship with another earth sign (Taurus, Virgo, or Capricorn) can have staying power, depending on what you want out of the relationship.

Around October 21 through November 20, you will become much more social and very much in demand, entertaining more and being entertained more. If you already have an ongoing relationship, now is the time it can become a real partnership. If you don't have a man on your arm now, this is a good time to look and find that someone special. Do be sure to always look your very best at all times, especially on Fridays. Friday will always be a very lucky day for you, so turn it to your advantage and go out on the town.

As you approach the colder months of November and December, it is a good time to ask, or look for, support. Surprisingly, a Sagittarius, a foreigner, or a teacher could come to your aid—physically, mentally, emotionally, or financially. If support is what you really need in a relationship (and please be honest with yourself), then ask, because if you don't, it could be a year before you have another chance.

The first month of winter, December 21 through January 20, may be a good time to get away. Vacations are necessary, and it could be very lucky for you if you plan a trip to Ireland. Don't forget to kiss the Blarney stone; you can then open up a conversation with the question, "Have you ever kissed the Blarney stone?" Since you are in Ireland, allow yourself some time for shopping in Dublin. You never know what or who you might meet when you explore the surrounding countryside with its castles, its pubs, and its terribly sexy men. Ireland is sure to put the bloom of the rose in your cheeks and the blarney on your lips! If you wish to stay a little closer to home, but still want a lucky spot, keep St. Louis in mind. St. Louis is called "The Gateway to the West," and the St. Louis Arch looks like a silver version of a leprechaun's magic rainbow. Perhaps you might take a Capricorn friend along. You can show him how to loosen up and have fun, and he can show you things you never dreamed of.

February 21 to March 20 is a time for old friends and a time to make new ones. You may be asked to join a new group of people for a singular goal, or you could be invited to join a club or audition for a local repertory company. A Scorpio, Pisces, or Cancer native can show you the ropes, and it can be a mutually rewarding experience. You can enjoy each other's company because you have many things in common. He can show you how to find the silver lining in any gray cloud, and you can show him how to turn that silver lining into gold. (Well, you *are* one of the money signs.)

Being friends in a long-term partnership like marriage can create a very comfortable environment. A relationship in which each allows the other the courtesy of being loved and being themselves without petty jealousies, as opposed to a more exciting but otherwise risky relationship, is best for you.

Helen, a beautiful, dark-haired Taurus, and Tony, a Cancer, have such a relationship. They are friends first. Helen and Tony have their own interests and are willing to admire and acknowledge each other's talents and encourage each other to move forward. As one watches them from the sidelines, it is obvious that each is indeed the other's best friend.

YOUR COSMIC STAR

Below is a list of the different areas of personal concern and the significance that each plays in your life. How each corresponds to your own personalized Cosmic Star is explained. When the sun passes over each area in turn, that area of your life is highlighted for approximately one month. Knowing this can be very helpful to you when you want to make an important move. This is very valuable information to have when you need to coordinate your timing with decisive action or start a new project. You know that your cosmic year can easily be individualized. It begins with this year's birthday and ends with your next birthday.

By familiarizing yourself with each astrological area of your Cosmic Star, you will know what part of your life will be paramount and how best to take advantage of your positive qualities.

1. ♈ **YOURSELF** When the sun highlights Area 1, it accents your need to look and be at your best.

2. ♊ **MATERIAL POSSESSIONS** When the sun highlights Area 2, you become much more aware of your worth.

3. ♋ **ABILITY TO COMMUNICATE** When the sun highlights Area 3, you wish to exchange ideas with other people.

4. ♌ **HOME AND FAMILY** When the sun highlights Area 4, you would like to spend more time at home with your family.

5. ♍ **LOVE LIFE** When the sun highlights Area 5, what you would really like to do is just enjoy life.

6. ♎ **WORK** When the sun highlights Area 6, you must work hard for the things you want.

7. ♏ **MARRIAGE** When the sun highlights Area 7, other people could be ready to make a commitment.

8. ♐ **SUPPORT** When the sun highlights Area 8, you may need help.

9. ♑ **TRAVEL** When the sun highlights Area 9, you find good luck on the road.

10. ≈≈   CAREER When the sun highlights Area 10, career moves can now go public.

11. ♓   FRIENDS When the sun highlights Area 11, you meet new people and make new friends.

12. ♈   THE END When the sun highlights Area 12, everything becomes known.

HOW TO USE YOUR COSMIC STAR

The easy-to-use Cosmic Star will help you to personalize your own chart by using your birthday as a starting point. I will begin by showing you where and how your cosmic year begins.

The points of the star move in a counterclockwise direction. Each point represents approximately one month. To make it personally yours, place your birthday at the point marked 1 ♉. Then, moving down again in a counterclockwise direction, place the next month and your birthday at point 2 ♊, and so forth, placing the same day and the next month at each point, until all the points are captioned.

As the year moves along, you can visualize how the sun's transits over these points each month will affect your life. You are now in a better position to anticipate major changes and capitalize on any new opportunities that could present themselves.

If you were born at the end of one sign or at the beginning of another, then turn to Appendix A on page 115, to find out exactly what constellation the sun was moving through at the time of your birth. To check how I individualized my own Cosmic Star, turn to Appendix B on page 125.

Taurus

April 21 – May 20

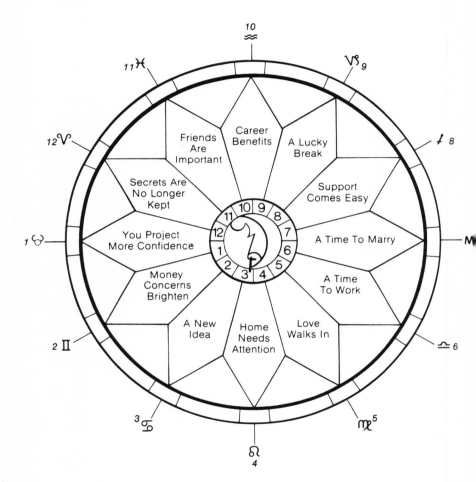

10 ≈

11 ♓

♑ 9

12 ♈

♐ 8

Friends Are Important

Career Benefits

A Lucky Break

Secrets Are No Longer Kept

Support Comes Easy

1 ♉

You Project More Confidence

A Time To Marry

M

Money Concerns Brighten

A Time To Work

2 ♊

A New Idea

Home Needs Attention

Love Walks In

♎ 6

3 ♋

♍ 5

♌ 4

Gemini

Only the excitement of a Gemini woman could bring spring to a close. It is hard to believe that any Gemini woman could have trouble finding a man. But maybe not, because you are looking for just the right man. You will never have trouble attracting attention. You might encounter problems because you really hate to be tied down to one man. Life is too short, and you want to live and experience it all. You are witty, funny, and dynamic, and how does any man catch a sunbeam in his hand? As you dance through your life, you draw some of the most fascinating, interesting people and some of the more exciting, outrageous opportunities into your orb. You have never been known to turn down an exciting offer. Sometimes that reckless, daredevil streak gets you into so much mischief that your more conservative sisters have to come to your rescue. Admittedly, they don't mind, because secretly they wish they could abandon themselves and let go the way you do. Invariably someone asks, "Why?" You answer, "Because I never tried it before." You never lack for attention or excitement.

This ability to generate excitement is quite an attention-getter, and some men are fascinated by this. You never slow down and you hardly ever look back. What kind of man can keep up with your games? Why, one who knows games that you would like to learn, of course.

Instinctively, men like you and you like them. But you need a man who will not tie you down. You need one who will allow you your freedom but also be willing to join you in a sparring session. And he should be interested in sports, since you love to spend lots of time outdoors.

Because you were born under the constellation Gemini and are an air sign ruled by the planet Mercury, you will always be on the move, slowing down only to learn something new, then moving on to greener pastures. Boredom is your worst enemy. It is very hard for you not to become bored with routine and people. There must always be something new for you to explore in order to keep you interested. You make friends easily, and a stranger does not remain a stranger for long. You are a good listener, but your repertoire of interesting little anecdotes and stories piques people's interest and holds them spellbound.

Did you know that a great number of models, like Brooke Shields and Marilyn Monroe, were born under the sign of Gemini? Like most models, your entrances are one of your strong points. You walk in with a total air of confidence and proceed to talk about "this funny thing that happened to me on my way over here." You have the best repertoire of opening lines of any sign in the zodiac and are never at a loss for words. Within the first ten minutes you have everyone in the room eating out of your hand, begging for more. When you do make your entrance or just happen to be showing off one of your many talents, stand tall and make sure you position yourself in the most elevated position possible. Even though you might be tall, you usually have a small, delicate appearance, so always stand straight and tall. It goes without saying that you can stand taller on a pedestal. I might add that your exits aren't your forte, because secretly you hate for the party to end.

Although you are great in person, you also make quite an impression over the telephone. Learning to use the telephone for a Gemini had to be the start of a lifelong love affair. You know how to use it to intrigue and entice your captive audience. When writing a letter, you know just what to say. Any form of communication is where you will be remembered, whether writing a cover letter, introducing the evening news, or just telling a funny story. This is one place where you will have no peers—everyone wants to listen to you.

While you talk, you gesture to make the story more animated. People focus on your hands, so take time out to give yourself a manicure. Use a brightly colored nail polish and never let your nails look chipped or unappealing. It is all part of the overall picture. It is the kind of effect you want when you are expressing yourself and want to make a point. You use those brightly colored, eye-catching nails when directing attention to someone or something. Your audience is compelled to follow where your fingertips lead. A word of caution: nervousness can cause you to bite your nails down to the quick or to smoke. Smoking can leave a stain on your fingers, burn holes in your clothes, and leave spots on your lungs. Nail biting can be painful, not to mention all those snagged nylons or pantyhose you have to replace. Gemini rules the hands, so be sure to take good care of them. It wouldn't hurt also to drink some gelatin to strengthen those nails.

When it comes to jewelry, you wrote the book. You have lots of it; something to go with everything you own. Might I suggest you invest in a few pieces of really good jewelry, preferably a ring or two, or three, to go on your always-in-motion fingers. Basically, you love junk jewelry and you want one of everything in every color, to match a particular outfit or whatever personality you want to project at the time. Again, the ring is your most important piece of jewelry. With it you let your hands weave their magic spell, fascinating and almost hypnotizing your man. The deep, dark green of a tourmaline or the fascinating watermelon stone (a two-colored tourmaline) with its dual colors will mirror the duality of your personality. Besides, what interesting stones to speculate on.

The Gemini native has always enjoyed the reputation of being a sharp dresser, but one must admit that vanity plays a key role in your final selection. You love to learn, and learning which colors and styles look best on you can be a lot of fun. Then, after all this studying and learning, you make it seem so simple, just as if you casually tossed on your clothes. Fads are a way of life for you, but you create them rather than follow them. You just can't wait to get your hands on something you have never seen before. A word of warning: don't spend lots of money on clothes, even though you enjoy them, because you have a habit of getting tired of them easily. Put that bargain-hunting sense of yours to work. Although you appreciate quality as well as quantity, if you were forced to choose one over the other you would usually opt for the quantity. You live with the belief that if one is good, two is better.

Like springtime, you like the crisp, clean-cut look. Perhaps you even like to mix and match the colorful sportswear sets you wear, which gives you much more flexibility and a variety of different outfits. I bet that you are an avid fan of the modern look, as well as a secret reader of *The Preppy Handbook*. Even your sneakers are coordinated. Only buy well-fitting, comfortable shoes that are fashionable too. Ill-fitting shoes not only slow you down, they can also bring on physical ailments. Now, off to fun and games. You can forget about how you look, because we both know you look wonderful.

I almost forgot to mention Gemini's lucky color. You look good in almost any color, but Gemini's personal colors are in the yellow family. The cheerful color of sunshine, lemon, and the pale yellow of butter all add up to a blending streak of sunlight rushing on by. More adventurous ladies have added a dash of pink to create a little more fun and a lot more flash, and they have encircled all of it with rhinestones for that madcap look.

As you are leaving the department store in a mad rush to get somewhere, don't forget to pick up a nice, fresh, clean cologne, like Lavender, Jean Naté, Love's Baby Soft, or just plain Babe. Try to get one of those little perfume samples to put in your emergency kit, along with a nail file, a bottle of clear nail polish (for your nails or to dab on a run in your pantyhose), an electric curling iron, a toothbrush and tube of toothpaste—because who knows where you will be tomorrow?

Wednesday is your day. Wednesday is the day you will meet success, the day to start any new venture, and just an all-around lucky day for you.

It is also a good day to look for those bargains you are so famous for.

People born during this period usually love crowds, and the more people involved, the luckier Geminis appear to be. The more you become involved in putting on a fair or a carnival, the more you increase your chances of meeting Mr. Right. As the sun passes over your birthday (May 21–June 20), you are more inclined to show off your many talents. One talent you possess is that you are an outrageous flirt who usually has more than one man going at a time, "just to keep things interesting," you might add. Just between us, I doubt you would readily admit to it unless you had to or were caught, whichever the case may be.

As the sun leaves your own sign, you will discover that you have made some very important, positive changes in your way of life. Three months later, when the sun enters Libra (September 21–October 20), you are ready to have some fun. You are going to want to match wits with a person as intelligent as you. This time it could be the real thing, or it could be a time when you are most apt to get yourself into mischief. What kind of mischief? Why, there may be so many men vying for your favors that if you don't write everything down, you could get your wires crossed. I would hate to see you call the right man by the wrong name! Perhaps it might be that nice, gentle Libran with a twinkle in his eye, or that fascinating Aquarian whom you just can't seem to pin down, or another Gemini who turns out to be a soul mate. Whichever one you choose, he will never be dull. Lynn, a cute, vivacious Gemini realtor, chose a good-looking Libran, and I would say, as an observer of human nature, that their life together is definitely not dull.

Time marches on, and when the sun enters Sagittarius (November 21– December 20) you start asking yourself what the attraction is. Everyone else is settling down and making a commitment, and maybe, just maybe, you are feeling a little bit left out. Making a commitment can enhance the fun in some romantic relationships. Be on the lookout. This time Mr. Right could come waltzing into your life. It opens up some fascinating possibilities for both of you.

The holiday season is here (December 21–January 20), and if ever you needed support, it is now. As unlikely as it seems, a Capricorn could come to your aid. It has to be one of the most unusual combinations in the zodiac, but it works. Gemini has the ideas and Capricorn has the know-how and drive. Who can argue with success?

Who would guess that in January or February you would be ready to go on vacation? All the holiday parties are over and the weather isn't that great. People seem to be staying home more, so why stick around? It would be worth your while to invest in a language class, or become part of an overseas exchange program where you can visit someone else's home or vice versa. If you have a choice, your best bet would be Belgium, and you must spend a few days' layover in London, where you can recover from jet lag. Many Geminis are bilingual and have the ability to learn a new language quite easily.

If international travel does not fit into your schedule this year, then perhaps a quick trip to the West Coast and a breathtaking view of San Francisco's Golden Gate Bridge will fit the bill. You just might leave your heart in San Francisco! Many Geminis who move to the Bay Area swear it was the luckiest move they ever made.

Spring puts in an appearance around March 21, and as it rolls around you meet and make some very interesting friends. Gemini women claim lots of men friends, such as an on-the-go Aries who adds spice to your life, or a good-looking Leo who makes no real demands on you. So consider a friend who won't tie you down. This could be the deal of the century.

YOUR COSMIC STAR

Below is a list of the different areas of personal concern and the significance that each plays in your life. How each corresponds to your own personalized Cosmic Star is explained. When the sun passes over each area in turn, that area of your life is highlighted for approximately one month. Knowing this can be very helpful to you when you want to make an important move. This is very valuable information to have when you need to coordinate your best timing with decisive action or start a new project. You know that your cosmic year can easily be individualized. It begins with this year's birthday and ends with your next birthday.

By familiarizing yourself with each astrological area of your Cosmic Star, you will know what part of your life will be paramount and how best to take advantage of your positive qualities.

1. ♊ YOURSELF When the sun highlights Area 1, it accents your need to look and be at your best.

2. ♋ MATERIAL POSSESSIONS When the sun highlights Area 2, you become much more aware of your worth.

3. ♌ ABILITY TO COMMUNICATE When the sun highlights Area 3, you wish to exchange ideas with other people.

4. ♍ HOME AND FAMILY When the sun highlights Area 4, you would like to spend more time at home with your family.

5. ♎   **LOVE LIFE** When the sun highlights Area 5, what you would really like to do is just enjoy life.

6. ♏   **WORK** When the sun highlights Area 6, you must work hard for the things you want.

7. ♐   **MARRIAGE** When the sun highlights Area 7, other people could be ready to make a commitment.

8. ♑   **SUPPORT** When the sun highlights Area 8, you may need help.

9. ♒   **TRAVEL** When the sun highlights Area 9, you find good luck on the road.

10. ♓   **CAREER** When the sun highlights Area 10, career moves can now go public.

11. ♈   **FRIENDS** When the sun highlights Area 11, you meet new people and make new friends.

12. ♉   **THE END** When the sun highlights Area 12, everything becomes known.

HOW TO USE YOUR COSMIC STAR

The easy-to-use Cosmic Star will help you to personalize your own chart by using your birthday as a starting point. I will begin by showing you where and how your cosmic year begins.

The points of the star move in a counterclockwise direction. Each point represents approximately one month. To make it personally yours, place your birthday at the point marked 1 ♊ . Then, moving down again in a counterclockwise direction, place the next month and your birthday at point 2 ♋, and so forth, placing the same day and the next month at each point until all the points are captioned.

As the year moves along, you can visualize how the sun's transits over these points each month will affect your life. You are now in a better position to anticipate major changes and capitalize on any new opportunities that present themselves.

If you were born at the end of one sign or at the beginning of another, then turn to Appendix A on page 115 to find out exactly what constellation the sun was moving through at the time of your birth. To check how I individualized my own Cosmic Star, turn to Appendix B on page 125.

Gemini

May 21 – June 20

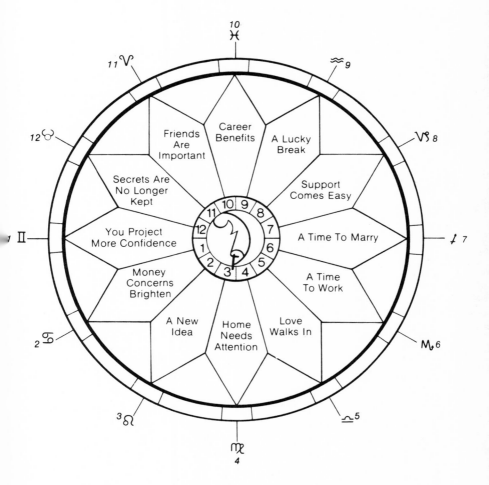

10 ♓

11 ♈

♒ 9

12 ♉

♑ 8

Friends Are Important

Career Benefits

A Lucky Break

Secrets Are No Longer Kept

Support Comes Easy

I ♊

You Project More Confidence

A Time To Marry

♐ 7

Money Concerns Brighten

A Time To Work

2 ♋

A New Idea

Home Needs Attention

Love Walks In

♏ 6

3 ♌

♎ 5

♍
4

4

Cancer

My dear sister, you are a child of the moon and one of the most feminine women in the zodiac. The moon, your ruler, has seen fit to give you a very dreamy look and the ability to easily attract men. Best of all, once a man becomes interested in you, he stays interested. Moon children are considered the most maternal and nurturing people in the zodiac. You always have a kind word to say to everybody, and you of all people know the damage a thoughtless, unkind word can do. Cancer natives are always there to lend a sympathetic ear to any sad story and give "tea and sympathy" when needed. You must use a little caution, though, because you can easily be taken advantage of, and therefore can easily be hurt.

When it comes to the type of man you want to attract, he should meet certain specifications. First, he should love children and be the type of man whom you would like to father your children, but he should also *be* a father to them, too. Next, he should be a good provider. Last, and this is probably the most important thing of all, he should love you and only you. These traits in a man are not only what you desire, but are what you deserve. Don't ever settle for anything less.

Unlike your Gemini sister who can make her grand entrance and get attention, you have the simple ability to just plain attract men—important men—into your orb. For example, Princess Diana just happened to catch Prince Charles's eye; the Empress Josephine had Napoleon wrapped around her little finger; and President Ronald Reagan still enjoys Nancy's company after many years of marriage. All Cancer natives are beautiful. You know how to endear yourself because of your positive vibrations, your sentimentality, your refined manners, and your sensuality.

Basically rather shy, the moon maiden is extremely sexy without even realizing it. Some men can easily be attracted to the woman who is the life of the party, but most men would rather not compete. There are many men who feel intimidated and threatened by these women and find them very hard to talk to. But not to you. You instinctively know when people are uncomfortable. All you have to do is smile at him in that knowing way of yours and all of a sudden you are approachable. An instant bond or rapport has been established. The secret to your overall success is that you know how to make yourself accessible. Men who were asked this one simple question, "What first attracted you to your mate, or lover?" answered, "She smiled at me and I knew. . . ." How simple the answer, and yet many women still don't know that this act of human kindness can get them the man they want. This is one of your many secret weapons in the battle of the sexes—you really care.

Since you know how to attract men, I will tell you where you can find them. Always keep in mind your personal interests and go from there. If you love animals as much as most Cancer natives, then spend some time working at the A.S.P.C.A. or an animal shelter. You, like your sister Taurus, are designated as one of the money signs, but you refuse to believe it. Speaking of money: how about a course in real estate investment or on income tax saving, or how about joining an investment club? Even if you don't happen to have an extra million on hand, you do have the ability to attract money and men who have money, though you are willing to assume a low profile. You possess this one little-known facet—you bring out the best in people and they naturally want to please you. People love giving you things, especially since you know how to accept gifts graciously, and you also know how to make people feel that they gave you the perfect gift—because they did.

You don't miss much, do you? You go out after what you want with an unmatched discipline that gets you exactly what you were after, and this includes a man. Like your symbol, the crab, you never go directly after what you want—that is why you always get it. Kind of like a surprise.

Fashions change, but your sense of style encompasses the old styles mixed with the new. Your motto may be "The old ways are the best," but you prefer the conveniences of modern living. The look is what you are striving for. When a man looks at you, you want him to reminisce about a more genteel way of life and evoke happy memories of a more gracious time. One way to achieve this kind of illusion is with clothes, makeup, and perfume. Appeal not only to his sense of sight, but to all his senses.

Honestly, didn't you feel more comfortable and prettier when playing dress-up in your mother's or your grandmother's clothes? You always admired the intricate lines and the drape of the garments, as well as the touch of handmade lace or the unique appliqué with its fine stitchery. It was a very feminine look and you adore it, so why don't you wear it? You can pick up some fantastic clothes by prowling around antique stores, thrift shops, or secondhand shops. But if you hate the upkeep on the real thing (and believe me, there is a lot of upkeep), then add a personal touch, such as antique lace

or antique jewelry, to brand-new period clothes. Many designers and manufac-
turers are bringing back the old styles in new, easy-care fabrics. Look into it;
I think you will be pleasantly surprised.

Cancer rules your chest and your waist and therefore you should show off
your assets. As often as you can, you might want to wear an antique moon-
stone pendant or a long rope of pearls that descend toward your plunging
neckline. Perhaps you would rather show off your waist with a jeweled belt
or a silver belt buckle. Silver goes beautifully with all your summer clothes
and silver is your metal, just as pearls and moonstones are your touchstones.
Pearls go with everything, but for you they bring good luck, good health,
and good fortune. Wear a pearl next to your skin and it will glow. Pearls
will keep you in good health by always reminding you of happier times and
protecting you against sad ones. Opalescent colors, or iridescent colors like
sea-foam green or silver-gray, will always bring you a smile from good
fortune. A word of warning: although sea-foam green is a very fortunate color
for you, it also has a tendency to attract water-weight gain, so use it more
as an accessory color, or when it is important for you to attract money. When
you do choose your colors, be sure that they are in your color palette, so that
you can present a total picture. Your shoes should be gray or taupe, with
matching nylons, which will give you a long, leggy look and make you appear
taller than you really are. Handbags should be the same color or lighter than
your shoes, and should be in proper proportion to your size.

Spending time on your makeup can be worth your while. Learn to use
pearlized or iridescent colors to enhance and excite. Again, you are striving
for that soft, romantic glow. One way in which you can achieve this is to
learn how to contour and soften your features. Once your makeup is applied,
dust it all over with a little glaze or a duster, which will set your makeup
and also will glow in the dark. Men can't help but take a second look at a
girl whose face lights up and shines in the misty moonlight.

Let me make a suggestion. Try to keep some fresh, seasonal flowers in a
crystal vase in your bedroom. Surround yourself with flowers such as white
iris, white roses, white lilacs, or perhaps a small bouquet of white wood violets
that you picked yourself while on one of your evening walks. Wear them on
your clothes or put them in your hair. If you are ever down, they can help
lift your spirits, and if not, you will get a reputation for old-world gracious
living. Remember, your fresh flowers should never clash with your perfume.
You can use any of the floral scents like Tea Rose, Chanel No. 5, or Chanel
No. 22. All of these will help keep you tucked away in his memory just like
a summer's day—he can't help but remember.

Moon maidens do have a little problem with their weight, water weight that is, especially around the day of the full moon. Since you do, I would like to suggest that you watch your salt intake and drink plenty of water. The reason why I mention it at all is that one of the luckiest places in the world for you is the beach. Looking good in a bathing suit will only enhance your chances of getting noticed by the kind of man you would like to meet. Another way to keep your figure is for you to exercise. During the summer months, you can run on the beach, which is excellent for your legs, or you can swim, which will keep all of your muscles in shape and your entire body firmed up.

Mondays, or the moon's days, are days when you can change your luck for the better. This includes changing the outlook on your love life. Love can come upon you on a summer's day or on a moonlit eve, when any man can get caught by your magical spell and your lilting laughter. You have a very subtle way of getting even the sphinx to crack a smile.

When fall is winding down and the sun enters Scorpio (October 21– November 21) you may find the love of your life, whether he is another water sign (Cancer, Scorpio, or Pisces) or one of the other signs. It is sure to be a relationship based on passion and mutual attraction. This kind of love could spring up aboard one of the luxury liners heading for warmer climes, or on a college campus. I might suggest that any traveling done by water will prove very rewarding for you. When you see that gorgeous man you are dying to meet looking a little lost or confused, just do what comes naturally. Go up to him, smile, and say, "Can I help you?"

Serious relations develop from December 21 to January 20, with the more exciting relationships settling down into permanent ones and new relationships becoming the long-lasting kind. Jodi, a Cancer, met Dick, a handsome Capricorn, as the sun moved into Scorpio. Two years later, on January 4, he proposed. For all Cancer natives, this is the time lots of new people (important people) will enter your life. Although you love to entertain in your own home and people enjoy your hospitality, I would recommend that you accept some of the many invitations that come your way. By expanding your circle of friends, you increase your chances of meeting the man of your dreams. If, on the other hand, you are planning on marriage, or making a relationship more stable, now is the time to take steps to do it. Steps taken now usually last for a long time. Like Jodi, think about a Capricorn man—they make wonderful husbands. Dick married Jodi and they had a perfect little Gemini. Well, you can't argue with perfection. On the other hand, maybe with a Gemini you can.

Interestingly enough, an Aquarian could be a person who is waiting in the wings to ride to your rescue in time of great need. They have the habit of being in the right place at the right time, again and again. Although you may not have a whole lot in common with this air sign, remember that your well-being will be one of his main concerns.

It would be absolutely fabulous if you could get away for a vacation and leave the cold, dreary winter days behind in mid-February through mid-March. Do something adventurous, like taking an overseas trip to Holland, stopping in Amsterdam to check out the diamonds. Then, travel south to Venice and sample their gondolas and appreciate their men. Doesn't that all sound scrumptious?

Can't afford to take too much time off? Then drive to New Hampshire and try your hand at one of the winter sports—it could just change your luck. Overall, this is a great time to get away, and wherever you go, good luck is bound to follow.

In two months your solar year comes to an end. As the sun is moving through Taurus (April 21–May 20) you are going to find that many of your cherished goals are being reached. You find yourself wishing that you could share all your good fortunate with your friends. There is a new lift to your step, and you whistle a happy tune just because spring is here and you feel good. For every season there is a purpose. This is a time for friends, and a Taurus makes you an excellent friend. As you may have guessed, you share a common bond—you both are money signs. I know you two have a lot to talk about.

YOUR COSMIC STAR

Below is a list of the different areas of personal concern and the significance that each plays in your life. How each corresponds to your own personalized Cosmic Star is explained. When the sun passes over each area in turn, that area of your life is highlighted for approximately one month. Knowing this can be very helpful to you when you want to make an important move. This is very valuable information to have when you need to coordinate your best timing with decisive action or start a new project. You know that your cosmic year can easily be individualized. It begins with this year's birthday and ends with your next birthday.

By familiarizing yourself with each astrological area of your Cosmic Star, you will know what part of your life will be paramount and how best to take advantage of your positive qualities.

1. ♋   YOURSELF When the sun highlights Area 1, it accents your need to look and be at your best.

2.   ♌   MATERIAL POSSESSIONS When the sun highlights Area 2, you become much more aware of your worth.

3.   ♍   ABILITY TO COMMUNICATE When the sun highlights Area 3, you wish to exchange ideas with other people.

4.   ♎   HOME AND FAMILY When the sun highlights Area 4, you would like to spend more time at home with your family.

5.   ♏   LOVE LIFE When the sun highlights Area 5, what you would really like to do is just enjoy life.

6.   ♐   WORK When the sun highlights Area 6, you must work hard for the things you want.

7.   ♑   MARRIAGE When the sun highlights Area 7, other people could be ready to make a commitment.

8.   ♒   SUPPORT When the sun highlights Area 8, you may need help.

9.   ♓   TRAVEL When the sun highlights Area 9, you find good luck on the road.

10.   ♈   CAREER When the sun highlights Area 10, career moves can now go public.

11.   ♉   FRIENDS When the sun highlights Area 11, you meet new people and make new friends.

12.   ♊   THE END When the sun highlights Area 12, everything becomes known.

HOW TO USE YOUR COSMIC STAR

The easy-to-use Cosmic Star will help you to personalize your own chart by using your birthday as a starting point. I will begin by showing you where and how your cosmic year begins.

The points of the star move in a counterclockwise direction. Each point represents approximately one month. To make it personally yours, place your birthday at the point marked 1 ♋ . Then, moving down again in a counter-clockwise direction, place the next month and your birthday at point 2 ♌ , and so forth, placing the same day and the next month at each point until all the points are captioned.

As the year moves along, you can visualize how the sun's transits over these points each month will affect your life. You are now in a better position to

anticipate major changes and capitalize on any new opportunities that could present themselves.

If you were born at the end of one sign or at the beginning of another, turn to Appendix A on page 115, to find out exactly what constellation the sun was moving through at the time of your birth. To check how I individualized my own Cosmic Star, turn to Appendix B on page 125.

Cancer

June 21 – July 20

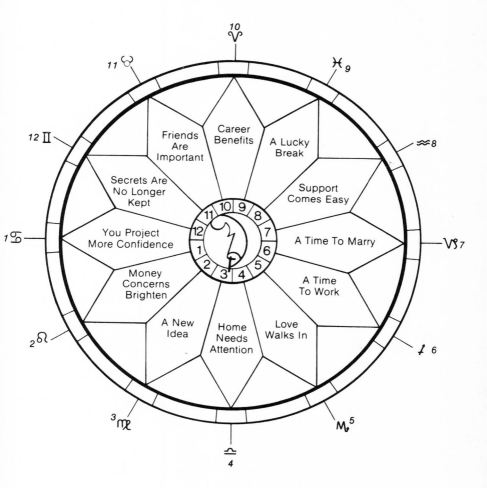

10 ♑

11 ♉

9 ♓

12 ♊

8 ≈

Friends Are Important

Career Benefits

A Lucky Break

Secrets Are No Longer Kept

Support Comes Easy

1 ♋

You Project More Confidence

A Time To Marry

7 ♑

Money Concerns Brighten

A Time To Work

2 ♌

A New Idea

Home Needs Attention

Love Walks In

6 ♐

3 ♍

5 ♏

4 ♎

 # Leo

Leo women are ruled by the sun and are called the lionesses of the zodiac because they always appear to be on the prowl. Wherever you go, you leave an easy-to-follow trail of fun and excitement. Your self-confident air and the commanding way you stand all go to make a real leader. Power and leadership are what naturally draw people to you, just like your namesake. As the sun is the center of our universe, so you are, and you enjoy being the center of attention. Nothing can be worse for a Leo than to be totally ignored. If you feel ignored, it's a sad sight to see a perky lioness on the skids. But then a friend calls up to lift your spirits and see how you are doing. You love people, you enjoy being with them, you like talking to them, and overall you are just an all-around people-oriented person. Remember, there are going to be times in your life when things aren't going to go as you would like. There will also be times when people are insensitive to your needs and your telephone hasn't rung all day. This is when you should be a little selfish and spend quiet time on yourself, ministering to your needs rather than to those of others. Tomorrow the telephone will start ringing again.

Men—what can I tell you about men that you don't already know? I can tell you what attitudes you should be looking for in the men you wish to have a relationship with. Everything considered, you need freedom in a relationship most of all. You need to feel completely comfortable. He must trust you and your judgment—no questions asked. (You hate to be cross-examined.) He had better not be the very jealous type, because you are one lady who is always in demand. Last but not least, he should go to the trouble of always looking good for you. You do it for him; therefore he should offer you the same courtesy.

It is time to take stock of some of your assets, and believe me, you have many of them to draw on. Entertaining is something you do very well. No wonder Leo natives enjoy the reputation of being the most gracious hostesses in the zodiac. Besides, you show real flair for putting the most fabulous people together. Just like Jackie Kennedy Onassis, you are a hostess whose invitations are never turned down.

Your beautiful hair is truly your crowning glory. Leo women are famous for their tresses and their coiffures, and you are no exception. Whether your hair is short or long, a trip to the beauty salon and a new hairstyle can work wonders for your morale. If, for example, your hairdresser suggests a shoulder-length style, it is because you can get a lot more mileage out of one good cut. At shoulder length, you can wear your hair up in a very daring or exotic look, or let it loose around your shoulders for a casual but seductive daytime look. If you decide to leave it long, then tie it back so that it is off your face when you play a few sets of tennis at the courts, or you can try putting your hair up in a topknot for a long round of golf at the club.

Perhaps, like Laura, a strawberry blond Leo coed, you may want a short, carefree, "go anywhere" style, easy to keep and easy to change. By the way, you make an excellent addition to any country or racquet club in your neighborhood. Not only do you enjoy lots of different sports and excel in many of them, you are also a great team player. Many times you will be asked to organize or lead, because you are a natural-born leader. You really care about the welfare of your contemporaries. You are generous with your time and magnanimous with your friends, which is one reason you have so many of them.

Leo natives in general are the real showmen in astrology. Your style is razzle-dazzle and keep them begging for more. Your motto seems to be "I don't care if we win or lose so long as everyone enjoys the show." Like Lucille Ball and Mae West, you are usually the star of the show. You love to shake your head and toss your hair on cue, at the precise moment when you know it will be most effective. You know exactly how your hair will fall, and that special look on your face will get you the desired result. It never fails to impress.

Leo, your sign, and the sun rule jewelers and goldsmiths. Therefore, your jewelry should always be made of gold (at least 14 karat). Your jewelry should be handcrafted or very distinctive, and never cheap. Good investments for Leo ladies are beautiful hair combs, or unique barrettes to hold your hair in place, or lots of necklaces to drape around your neck. Perhaps you could try something a little more daring, such as a wide gold bracelet to wear on your upper arm, like an Amazon queen. When choosing jewels, think about the ruby, which will always protect the wearer from the tyranny of others. Cat's-eyes, on the other hand, will give you the power to see through people's motives and will help you distinguish your friends from your enemies at first glance. Cat's-eyes are supposed to confer on their owner the ability to miss nothing and see everything, something a sun maiden continually strives for.

Like Coco Chanel, also a Leo, you love beautiful clothes because they are one way of expressing the many facets of your personality. Clothes are also a way of creating the image you would like to show the world at a particular time. One thing you must be concerned about is your habit of buying on impulse. Try to keep a basic plan for your wardrobe in mind, so that you can continually update your wardrobe and use everything you purchase. Take a suggestion from professional color consultants. When you go shopping for new clothes, cut a small swatch of material from the seams of those clothes you wish to match and keep it with you, so that you can match your new clothes with your present ones and not have to worry about buying the wrong color.

Lucky colors for Leo natives are the hues of summer—all the colors of gold, ranging from the palest straws to the true metallic golds. Wearing the colors of the sun will always bring the Leo golden girl good fortune. (Gold attracts gold.) Add an accessory or two in red and see what magic you can make.

When you start planning your wardrobe for the new season, be sure to include at least one wrap dress and one of those clingy little knits. When actually choosing your clothes, be sure to check the drape to see if they hang correctly on you. Your body is like that of a cat, and your clothes should fit and cling like a second skin. If you've got it, flaunt it. Show it off to its best advantage. (P.S. Every Leo should have a full-length mirror to preen in front of, and at least one fur coat hanging in her closet.) I have saved the best for last. Every Leo woman should have one backless dress for evening. It can be very provocative and leave a lot to the imagination. You want to keep them guessing and coming back for more. You love to give the element of surprise when you turn to leave, pivoting on your heels, giving everyone the thrill of seeing a plunging backless dress. It will make the men wish they had met you earlier and could stop you from leaving.

Most Leo women know how to apply makeup. Only two words of caution. First, use softer, less dramatic makeup during the daytime, and second, change your makeup if you get a tan. You are a sun worshipper, so again, be careful. Use the proper techniques and lotions to encourage a tan, not a burn.

Once you have settled on your look, add the matching scent. The fragrance that is supposed to attract the opposite sex is called musk oil. Look for colognes that feature it. Other perfumes you might want to add to your collection are Tigress, Vanderbilt, or one of the subtler, citrus-based fragrances. It all works to create just the statement you wish to make.

All Leo natives love a get-together or being seen at the newest hot spot in town. The trick is to see and be seen. Not only are parties lucky for you, but if they happen to be on a Sunday, so much the better. Every Sunday will renew your luck. When you finally arrive (usually fashionably late), after having practiced your entrance in front of a mirror all day, the first thing you do is look for a friend who appears to know just about everybody. They are so happy you have come, they can't wait to introduce you to everyone. You, on the other hand, allow them to make the introductions, and on first meeting, you choose to grace everyone with a dazzling smile, a toss of your head, and a polite "Hello" until you have got the lay of the land. Now you are ready to venture out on your own.

The Leo sign means love in astrology, and you can't seem to live without it. If you aren't in love now, then as the sun enters Sagittarius (November 21–December 20) you can find happiness. It will be the kind of situation where you fall madly, passionately in love. Make use of all the parties and holiday festivities that are coming your way. Remember: timing is everything. I would not put it past you to come out of this period trying to juggle two or more love interests at one time. Lucky you. Some of us find it hard to handle one relationship, but you manage. Leo natives love to live dangerously. Yours is an exciting life, and if you choose love with another fire sign (Aries, Leo, or Sagittarius) it can be even more exciting.

In January or February you could find that settling down with one person is constantly on your mind. You may just have met your match—the person you will eventually marry and spend the rest of your life with. You are ready to spend long hours thinking and talking about what you want from a relationship and what you are willing to give. At last you are ready to listen to what a prospective partner wants and needs. A time for action, to give and get all the good things life has to offer. Your horizons broaden, and an Aquarian, or one of the other air signs (Gemini or Libra), is ready to follow your lead.

During the last month of winter (February 21–March 20) you are going to find help if you need it. If you have been having a rough time finding someone to support you, now will be a time of sheer inspiration when you, or someone else, can come up with some very creative solutions. The solutions may sound crazy, but if anyone can get them to work, you can. Not only will they work, but you may get support from a very unusual individual. As unlikely a combination as Pisces and Leo is, Pisces will throw all of their resources and support behind you and your endeavors. Pisces and Leo—yes, it is an unusual combination, but they have certain resources at their fingertips that can hold a union together for years.

When the sun crosses over the equator, returning spring to us, you come alive with lots of new plans for the future. You are renewed, as all living things are. For some of you, this renewal will be spurred on by a much-needed vacation. Maybe you will travel to exotic places like the jungles of India and shop for elephant-tusk jewelry in the marketplaces of Bombay. Perhaps you will retrace the grandeur that once was France by visiting the palace at Versailles, where you can imagine a long-forgotten world when your every wish was a command. Speaking of wishes, perhaps you would rather live dangerously and take a risk by going to one of the gambling meccas of the world, where bed and board are low and the stakes are high. Many times you will come out a big winner, but there is always a chance you could lose, so never gamble more than you can afford to lose.

On a final note, friendship is something very precious to a Leo native. A man can be a great lover, but if he is not a friend, he is not the right man for you. If he asks you to give up any of your friends for him, you can be devastated and very lonely. You love your friends and they love you. The Leo woman is extremely loyal and not a fair-weather friend. One need only call you and you will be there, no matter what the emergency. Most of your best friends are active, intelligent, creative individuals who like to share new ideas with you. You are known by the company you keep, so surround yourself with people from the art world, such as artists, musicians, writers, actors, actresses, and the ever-present critics. Half the fun of friendship is the exchange of ideas and the creation of new ones. A long-term relationship based on mutual trust and admiration has staying power.

YOUR COSMIC STAR

Below is a list of the different areas of personal concern and the significance that each plays in your life. How each corresponds to your own personalized Cosmic Star is explained. When the sun passes over each area in turn, that area of your life is highlighted for approximately one month. Knowing this can be very helpful to you when you want to make an important move. This is very valuable information to have when you need to coordinate your best timing with decisive action or start a new project. You know that your cosmic year can easily be individualized. It begins with this year's birthday and ends with your next birthday.

By familiarizing yourself with each astrological area of your Cosmic Star, you will know what part of your life will be paramount and how best to take advantage of your positive qualities.

1.　♌　YOURSELF When the sun highlights Area 1, it accents your need to look and be at your best.

2. ♍ MATERIAL POSSESSIONS When the sun highlights Area 2, you become much more aware of your worth.

3. ♎ ABILITY TO COMMUNICATE When the sun highlights Area 3, you wish to exchange ideas with other people.

4. ♏ HOME AND FAMILY When the sun highlights Area 4, you would like to spend more time at home with your family.

5. ♐ LOVE LIFE When the sun highlights Area 5, what you would really like to do is just enjoy life.

6. ♑ WORK When the sun highlights Area 6, you must work hard for the things you want.

7. ♒ MARRIAGE When the sun highlights Area 7, other people could be ready to make a commitment.

8. ♓ SUPPORT When the sun highlights Area 8, you may need help.

9. ♈ TRAVEL When the sun highlights Area 9, you find good luck on the road.

10. ♉ CAREER When the sun highlights Area 10, career moves can now go public.

11. ♊ FRIENDS When the sun highlights Area 11, you meet new people and make new friends.

12. ♋ THE END When the sun highlights Area 12, everything becomes known.

HOW TO USE YOUR COSMIC STAR

The easy-to-use Cosmic Star will help you to personalize your own chart by using your birthday as a starting point. I will begin by showing you where and how your cosmic year begins.

The points of the star move in a counterclockwise direction. Each point represents approximately one month. To make it personally yours, place your birthday at the point marked 1 ♌ . Then, moving down again in a counterclockwise direction, place the next month and your birthday at point 2 ♍, and so forth, placing the same day and the next month at each point until all the points are captioned.

As the year moves along, you can visualize how the sun's transits over these points each month will affect your life. You are now in a better position to

anticipate major changes and capitalize on any new opportunities that could present themselves.

If you were born at the end of one sign or at the beginning of another, turn to Appendix A on page 115 to find out exactly what constellation the sun was moving through at the time of your birth. To check how I individualized my own Cosmic Star, turn to Appendix B on page 125.

Leo

July 21 – August 20

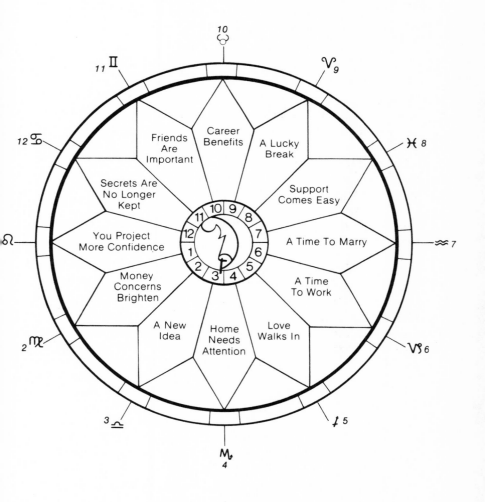

Career Benefits

Friends Are Important

A Lucky Break

Secrets Are No Longer Kept

Support Comes Easy

You Project More Confidence

A Time To Marry

Money Concerns Brighten

A Time To Work

A New Idea

Home Needs Attention

Love Walks In

6

Virgo

Lady Virgo, your symbol is the virgin waiting for her lover to come. Are you waiting for your knight in shining armor to sweep you off your feet and rescue you from the everyday world? Well if you are, he had better be witty, exciting, and creative, and he must fulfill your every secret desire and your wildest fantasies. (Admit it, you do have some pretty wild fantasies.) But being the lady you are, no one would ever guess that beneath that cool exterior beats the heart of a passionate, wild romantic. If ever a lady could bring out the animal in a man, you sure could—that is, once you have captured him.

Good-looking men are a dime a dozen, but looks aren't everything. You appreciate a nice-looking man, but physical attributes are not what ultimately impress you. You look beyond the facade and can see the real person, not the trimmings or trappings. But tread softly—sometimes you tend to magnify the positive and eliminate the negative, and that can be a big mistake. Just because you are so honest and aboveboard doesn't mean that everyone else is. It is very hard for you to believe that others could deliberately deceive you. If for some reason you become disillusioned in love, it could be very painful for you. If, on the other hand, you do not allow yourself to vent your disappointment, then it may become very hard for you ever to really trust anyone again. Do not punish someone else who may want to get to know you better, or someone who may love you, despite the indiscretions of another unthinking, careless person who could not appreciate what he had.

Virgo women are among the kindest, gentlest, most beautiful women in the world. The list of beautiful Virgo women reads like a "Who's Who" of the entertainment world: Raquel Welch, Sophia Loren, Jacqueline Bisset, Greta Garbo, Anne Bancroft, and Lauren Bacall, to name just a few. However, a Virgo woman would rather be loved for her mind, for her wit, and for being herself than for her physical attributes. A Virgo woman can truly be called a real woman. Sometimes you appear to other people as rather distant because of your quiet, shy ways. On the other hand, once a man has made contact with you, you soon become an old-fashioned challenge to him—one he must court in order to win. If he is a gentleman and he does win, he will receive a prize beyond measure: a woman who can love and delight him for the rest of his life.

Meeting men can be a lot of fun and very easy if you just use a little practical know-how. One way to meet men is to pinpoint groups of men who have a similar social background and tastes, interests, hobbies, careers, likes, and dislikes similar to yours. Start with a common interest. One such interest could be centered on small pets or other animals. (The sign of Virgo rules small house pets.) The next time you are interested in acquiring a pet, think pedigree. Once you decide on your pet, join a local club that specializes in your breed. If it happens to be a dog, look into the possibility of sending it to obedience classes, the kennel club, or showing your pet locally. Show your pet just for the fun of it, to expand your circle of friends—and your pick of the litter could be a big winner. Some animals have been known to increase their owner's bank account. If buying an expensive animal is not in your stars, then you could get a very lovable pet from the A.S.P.C.A. or a local animal shelter. While you are there, you may want to volunteer a few hours a month for a very good cause. Who knows? Perhaps a pet could bring you together!

Pets, libraries, museums, and money houses will always bring the Virgo native luck, so next time you are standing in a long line at the bank, look to see who is next to you.

Virgos have considerable organizational skills and artistic talent. Why not take an art appreciation class at one of your favorite museums, or become an artist yourself? If you are unsure of your talent (most Virgos are extremely talented), take an art class and be prepared to show your work at the nearest artists' guild. If none of these suggestions appeals to you, then be daring and bold—sign up for a seminar in personal business financing. You also have good sense where money is involved.

One of your least-known attributes is your high intellect. Even if you don't pursue a formal education, you never stop studying those things that interest you. Many Virgos decide to return to school after being away for many years. The diploma may not be the driving force behind it, but rather your insatiable need to learn. Whether you go back to school for a diploma or just for the fun of it, either way it makes the quality of your life better. You can meet lots of people who share many of the same interests as you.

You are often referred to as a "cool, elegant loner" who would almost never be found going out on a blind date. You can get your own man, thank you very much. Again, you show a discriminating taste that invariably leans toward brains and wit rather than muscle and brawn. You know right down to the very penny what you are worth on the open market, and you will not settle for one cent less.

Attracting a man's attention and then freezing that moment in time is going to be a hard lesson for you to learn. Men do notice you, but sometimes you come off as untouchable, so you get passed over for one of your more open sisters. Next time, take a lesson from your Cancer sister: if he looks interesting and you would like to meet him, catch his eye by smiling at him. Then follow up by getting a friend to make the more formal introduction if he loses you in the crowd. This is only one technique that shy little you can use anytime and anywhere.

Virgo is ruled by the planet Mercury. Mercury rules your physical well-being. Always remember: you, more than any other sign of the zodiac, are susceptible to uncomfortable situations. Your mental health governs your physical health and that in turn governs your outward appearance. So keep worry to a minimum and surround yourself with positive vibrations. I could tell you to stop worrying, but I know you and you can't help it. Choose Wednesday as your day to relax—the one day you use just for you. You will be rejuvenated and ready to accept lucky opportunities that come into your aura. Perhaps you might try a high-fiber diet, coupled with easy exercise, such as meditation or yoga, to help you slow down and take it easy.

Virgo natives have a reputation for being very loyal, even to your brand of makeup. You hate to throw it away if there is even a little bit of your favorite color left. Makeup does get old and out of style, and after a while some of it can affect your health, as it can harbor germs. If you don't update your makeup and your look, it could make you appear older than you are. Learn how to contour your face, using the right colors for you, by asking one of your Aquarian or Libran friends. Find out how to get a more natural look by using different brushes to play up your eyes, as well as your naturally good bone structure. An emergency kit should always contain a toothbrush and toothpaste (to brush after every meal), a blusher, mascara, eye shadow (green or brown), a needle and thread (just in case), and an extra pair of nylons or pantyhose.

Talking about nylons—be good to your feet and they will be good to you. Throw out all your old, run-down shoes. I know; you hate to throw out anything, but old, ill-fitting shoes are not only unsightly, they can be hazardous. Massage your feet and hands with a softening lotion after a long day and I guarantee you will feel so good you will want to go dancing.

Your colors are the deep hues of late summer. The range of colors goes from the shade-tree greens to the dusty cocoas and seaweed brown and includes all shades of tan and beige. Wearing colors that are governed by your ruler tends to bring you lots of luck and compliments. One day I noticed that Nancy, my boss, who also just happens to be a Virgo, wore a beautifully tailored brown skirt, a simple but elegant cocoa silk blouse, and very expensive brown pumps, all topped off with a sporty little mink jacket. She felt great, looked terrific, and had a simply marvelous day. The day she hired me she was wearing a warm taupe cardigan with a matching plaid shirt (and that was one lucky day for both of us!).

The clothes that you choose for yourself are expensive, of high quality, and you always gravitate toward the classics, such as a real Chanel suit or that little black dress that never goes out of style. If you turn that little black dress into a soft, beige wool, it would brighten up your whole look. Never let your clothes look out of date. Whenever possible, add accessories and colors that keep your clothes in style. For convenience, add a pair of slacks or a well-fitting pair of trousers to an old tweed jacket, and finish it all off with a matching silk shirt and a pair of chocolate kidskin gloves.

If you are one of the millions of women who wear glasses, update them every few years. First, because you should have an eye examination every year; second, because frame styles change; and third, because you would hate to miss anything!

If you are interested in promoting good health, wear a sapphire. If you are more interested in attracting good luck, however, wear either a smoky topaz or an antique cameo. Both will force providence to smile on you, and good fortune will follow.

The *pièce de résistance,* the final touch to set you permanently in his mind forever, is the fragrance he can't forget. Scents touch our minds and linger long after you are gone. You want to choose one that is subtle, fresh, and tells a man that what he sees is exactly what he gets—no games. Try the new fragrances Blazer, Lavender, or Sophia. All are made for you, and all are lovely.

When the seasons change, so do your opportunities. I suggest that, as a practical person, you capitalize on your opportunity to fall in love when the sun enters Capricorn (December 21–January 20). You could begin by making plans for the holidays that include lots of fun and surprises for those family members and friends who are closest to you. Go to all of the parties you have been invited to. Not only do people want you as a guest, but Mr. Right may be at one of those many functions, and you are not going to meet him if you don't make yourself available. Also, it could be a good time to take a vacation and get away from it all. Go off by yourself to get your second wind and think about the new year to come. You need not spend a lot of money. You could team up with another earth friend (Capricorn, Taurus, or another

Virgo) whose uncle has a cabin or a condominium somewhere you would like to go. It's just a good time to go off and have a wonderful time.

A month or so later, when the transiting sun enters Pisces (February 21–March 20), you will find that more people are entering your life and are here to stay. People you meet now are to be permanent additions in your life, as well as helpmates. Be alert. There is a good possibility that a man you meet now could be the one you would like to pledge your troth to. If, on the other hand, you are planning a wedding, then marry now while the sun lends an extra blessing to your union. You will find you can achieve incredible happiness in this relationship.

When spring comes, you may have to actively seek support. If you have been experiencing some difficulties, now is the time for action. "Seek and ye shall find—ask and ye shall receive." You usually are very self-sufficient and hate to ask for help from others. Most people are not mind readers, so if you need a little help, ask. All relationships are based on needed support or mutual need. No matter what it is you want, it will be available now if you just make your needs known.

Planning to do some traveling? If a little trip is in order, April or May could be just the right time for you to go. Virgos fare very well when traveling by land or by air. If you like the idea of adventure, then April in Paris is exhilarating. The European countryside is coming alive, and Switzerland or Greece weaves a magic all its own. Perhaps you might plan to take in the Cannes Film Festival while over there. Who knows who you could run into? And what a great opening line: "Didn't we meet at Cannes last year?"

Okay, practical Virgo—you will save your money to go next year, but you still want a fun but inexpensive vacation this year. Talk one of your water-sign friends (Cancer, Scorpio, or Pisces) into pooling resources and driving up to Boston and then to the Cape for a little history and a lot of sun. Not close enough? What about a long weekend in Washington, D.C., where you could rub elbows with the "Who's Who" of the political set? Still too far away? What about a trip to the West Coast and the California sunshine, Napa Valley, Lake Tahoe, Hollywood, and, of course, Disneyland? Any part of California will bring you the luck of the " '49ers." "There is gold in them thar hills," if you know what you are looking for. And all Virgos know what they are looking for.

YOUR COSMIC STAR

Below is a list of the different areas of personal concern and the significance that each plays in your life. How each corresponds to your own personalized

Cosmic Star is explained. When the sun passes over each area in turn, that area of your life is highlighted for approximately one month. Knowing this can be very helpful to you when you want to make an important move. This is very valuable information to have when you need to coordinate your best timing with decisive action or start a new project. You know that your cosmic year can easily be individualized. It begins with this year's birthday and ends with your next birthday.

By familiarizing yourself with each astrological area of your Cosmic Star, you will know what part of your life will be paramount and how best to take advantage of your positive qualities.

1. ♍ **YOURSELF** When the sun highlights Area 1, it accents your need to look and be at your best.

2. ♎ **MATERIAL POSSESSIONS** When the sun highlights Area 2, you become much more aware of your worth.

3. ♏ **ABILITY TO COMMUNICATE** When the sun highlights Area 3, you wish to exchange ideas with other people.

4. ♐ **HOME AND FAMILY** When the sun highlights Area 4, you would like to spend more time at home with your family.

5. ♑ **LOVE LIFE** When the sun highlights Area 5, what you would really like to do is just enjoy life.

6. ♒ **WORK** When the sun highlights Area 6, you must work hard for the things you want.

7. ♓ **MARRIAGE** When the sun highlights Area 7, other people could be ready to make a commitment.

8. ♈ **SUPPORT** When the sun highlights Area 8, you may need help.

9. ♉ **TRAVEL** When the sun highlights Area 9, you find good luck on the road.

10. ♊ **CAREER** When the sun highlights Area 10, career moves can now go public.

11. ♋ **FRIENDS** When the sun highlights Area 11, you meet new people and make new friends.

12. ♌ **THE END** When the sun highlights Area 12, everything becomes known.

HOW TO USE YOUR COSMIC STAR

The easy-to-use Cosmic Star will help you to personalize your own chart by using your birthday as a starting point. I will begin by showing you where and how your cosmic year begins.

The points of the star move in a counterclockwise direction. Each point represents approximately one month. To make it personally yours, place your birthday at the point marked 1 ♍ . Then, moving down again in a counter-clockwise direction, place the next month and your birthday at point 2 ♎ , and so forth, placing the same day and the next month at each point until all the points are captioned.

As the year moves along, you can visualize how the sun's transits over these points each month will affect your life. You are now in a better position to anticipate major changes and capitalize on any new opportunities that could present themselves.

If you were born at the end of one sign or at the beginning of another, turn to Appendix A on page 115 to find out exactly what constellation the sun was moving through at the time of your birth. To check how I individual-ized my own Cosmic Star, turn to Appendix B on page 125.

Virgo
August 21 – September 20

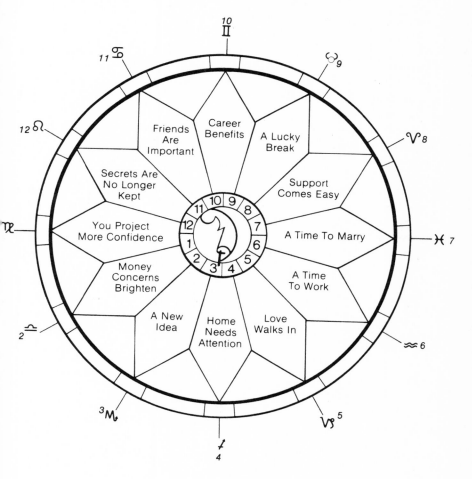

Career Benefits

Friends Are Important

A Lucky Break

Secrets Are No Longer Kept

Support Comes Easy

You Project More Confidence

A Time To Marry

Money Concerns Brighten

A Time To Work

A New Idea

Home Needs Attention

Love Walks In

7

Libra

The Libran woman has always been blessed by her ruling planet, Venus. She has been given grace, refinement, and good looks. Some of the world's most beautiful women, like Brigitte Bardot, Catherine Deneuve, and Carole Lombard, were born under Libra. Not only were you blessed with beauty, you were also given the ability to know just what to do with it. Your early life appeared to be just a rehearsal for when you grew up. You were the little girl who couldn't wait to learn how to put on makeup or wear high heels. Once you were allowed to wear makeup, you could spend hours looking over the latest fashion magazines to learn the proper technique for applying it. When you finally had the technique down pat, you knew how to accentuate your best features. Never again would you ever look anything but gorgeous.

Libran women have never had a problem finding men. It appears to be universally understood that Libran women are the best-loved women in the zodiac. But what should you be looking for in a man? Most important, he must appeal to you esthetically. In other words, he had better be good-looking, with a pleasant disposition, as well as being a sharp dresser. If he has none of these qualities, then he won't get a second chance. You have just too many men to choose among. A man who catches your eye is going to attract your attention. Once your interest has been piqued, then you want to be swept off your feet, romanced, wined, and dined in the style to which you have become accustomed. It has to be love with all the trimmings, trappings, and wrappings. Mother told you you shouldn't have to settle for anything less, and Daddy told you you were his little princess; therefore, you are entitled to be treated as such. One word of warning: steer clear of a jealous man or a man who wants to possess you body and soul. Although you may be flattered by his attention at first, it could become unpleasant very quickly. You are your own person, and if anyone tries to force his will on you, you are going to resent it. Save yourself some grief. In your first few years of dating, do not tie yourself down to one man—give them all a chance to enjoy your company. Discover what you like about each individual, have fun, and allow your taste in men to develop before you make up your mind. The really interesting thing about a Libran woman is that she can make a good match with just about any of the other signs, because she is so diversified.

Flirting can be fun, and you love to do it because it makes you feel so feminine when you get your own way. Librans are famous for their sweet dispositions, and yours helps you go far in this life. You are also reputed to be the diplomats of the world, and you learn early in life how to effect compromise between disgruntled playmates. Libran natives hate any kind of unpleasantness or nasty scene, so you will do just about anything to avoid a bitter confrontation or an out-and-out unkindness. This is why, as an adult, you could become the arbitrator in many disputes. It is agreed that you are always fair and can see both sides of the argument. You can then come up with an amicable solution that pleases everyone concerned. No wonder you have so many friends and adoring fans.

Sexy beyond belief (and you know you are), you really know how to enjoy your femininity. You manage to get every ounce of pleasure out of each day; you find poetry in the wind and pictures in the sunsets. Born with a natural charisma that draws people to you, you have the ability to open up a whole new social scene that consists of the most interesting people in the zodiac. Some people call it sophistication, some call it class, but whatever it is, you definitely have it. You enjoy the distinction of being able to travel in more than one social circle at a time and make yourself at home wherever you are. You find it easy to always put others at ease; you can make them feel comfortable in your presence. Besides, you can always find something exceptional about anybody you come in contact with. In other words, you make people feel important. This all goes to making you a delightful companion to have around.

A long time ago you discovered there was a definite difference between little boys and little girls. You enjoyed being a little girl because it had some definite advantages and benefits. One: you enjoyed all the attention from the boys, like having them carry your books home after school. Two: you especially liked the fact that boys usually pay for everything on a date. Most men consider you sweet and innocent, but you are not as innocent as you appear. When you see a man you would like to get to know a little better, then you plot your strategy. First you get his attention and then you have him right where you want him. You believe in the old saw "He chased her until she caught him." Although for you the chase and courtship are nice, it is not the big payoff. The ultimate joy is in the love you can share and the care you can give. A Libran's real fun begins when she has someone else she can share things with. Take Dorothy, a lovely Libran, who enjoys doing things with

Bob. Everything turns into a team effort. But she still can find time to share with her friends, especially me, and I love it because she is a fun lady to be with.

Nothing is ever simple with you. You are a complex person who does everything in a very well-thought-out, methodical manner. Not even your makeup is simple. You are always up on the latest, in hopes of improving on perfection. Libran women are renowned for their beautiful faces. They are reputed to have the most beautiful faces in the world. How could makeup improve on your bright, sparkling smile and your other attributes? It can only accentuate what you already have naturally. Libran skin is usually paler than most other complexions, and even at a young age you should get into the habit of daily cleansing, creaming, and moisturizing your skin as often as needed. It is one of your better features, and if you take care of it, it will take care of you by not divulging your age. Whether during the day or at night, be sure to wear some kind of foundation to protect delicate, exposed skin, and when your nose looks shiny use a little pressed powder. If you happen to be spending the evening with that special someone, dust your cheeks and eyelids with a little "stardust" to add an extra glow.

While we are on the subject of your skin, remember to take care of your hands and feet. Moisturize them whenever possible. Once in a while, treat yourself to a professional manicure. If and when you are forced to do housework, protect your hands by wearing rubber gloves (the kind with an absorbent cotton lining).

Most Librans love to shop. You keep a keen eye on the fashion scene and you always know what is "in." But I must add that your taste runs to the expensive one-of-a-kind items. It's not that you deliberately look for the hard-to-find pricey items—it's just that you have such great taste in clothes. You do not work for one particular look, but you like to cultivate and indulge your good taste by trying many different looks. It all works because you have a face and body that can carry it all off. Whatever the occasion, you stand out. Lace can be worn for afternoon tea, and then later a quick change into a butter-soft leather for evening, which others may find a bit unusual, but then, you have always managed to be a trendsetter and achieve a certain *je ne sais quoi.* It has been my experience that many Libran women design their own clothes, since they have so many distinct ideas on style and dress. If they can't find what they are looking for, then they may be forced to express their own style by making it.

Lady Luck will always smile on you when you wear one of the colors that Venus rules. Librans' colors are the tints and pastels of blue. You can wear everything from the conservative Wedgwood blue to the softer, cooler baby and powder blues—blue that mirrors the sky, light blue that is the color of a robin's egg. All of these are the first choices of the intellects, the educated, and the artists. Blue can also be a power color, such as navy blue. Navy blue gives you the ability to speak with authority and be listened to, even in the boardroom. So if you are looking for a power suit, choose a conservative navy blue, and for added inspiration wear a pink shirt (just to keep that feminine quality). Round out the look with a pair of navy shoes and a matching handbag. Now you are ready for anything.

"Diamonds are a girl's best friend," or so the song says, and the gems that will excite your imagination are of the pink variety. Along with pink diamonds, add coral and the fiery, fragile opal. Legend says that Venus, goddess of love and beauty, took such a fancy to the Libran native for services rendered that in their honor she created a gem the likes of which had never been seen on earth before. It was fashioned out of the most beautiful colors of the rainbow, and she called it an opal. The opal was to be worn as a symbol of her protection, and to ensure her edict she placed a curse on the newly created stone, so that if it was ever worn by anyone who was not in tune with the Libran vibrations, the stone would shatter, never to be held by another human being again. Fact or fiction—whichever it is—it will always bring you protection from misfortune.

Perfumes are a Libran's delight. They must be unusual, sensuous, expensive, and speak of the woman who wears them. Fleur de Fleurs, Enjoli, White Linen, and Love Wins are a few of the fragrances you might like to experiment with. Find a scent that reflects you and be sure it blends in with any fresh flowers you happen to surround yourself with. All Librans love flowers, and you especially like being surprised with a dozen pink roses. If no one buys them for you, you have been known to splurge and buy them for yourself, just because they were so pretty and they lifted your spirits.

Sunshine and beautiful fall days bring out the best in a Libran lady. During the day (preferably a Friday) you like to be taken out to lunch at some romantic hideaway by the man you love. Sometimes you even fancy yourself as the other woman. Not true. You have the ability to so capture a man's imagination, there is really no competition. You are the only woman in his heart. When night falls, our Libran lady could astonish us all by turning into a gypsy, who steals away in the night and clouds men's judgment, just for the fun of it.

Libran women were made to be loved, and you are no exception. After the holidays are over, between January 21 through February 20 love and excitement enter your life. While the rest of the world is recovering from the new year, you are getting your second wind. You drop a few pounds, look great, and receive lots of proposals—not necessarily a marriage proposal. If you are itching for some fun, take a vacation, or at least a long weekend to get away to some neat little romantic spot. Perhaps a weekend in Manhattan might be fun: catch a Broadway play, have lunch at the Russian Tea Room, or visit the Metropolitan Museum of Art. If you take advantage of some of the finer hotel offers of bed and breakfast, it could prove quite profitable in more ways than one. You may come home singing "New York, New York," if you come home at all.

After the sun passes the equator on March 21 and if you have met the man of your dreams, you may be ready to make that big commitment, or it could be the other way around. The man who dreams of you at night could walk into your life and be ready to say "I do." Right now, you are receptive to a one-on-one relationship, more than at any other time of the year. Remember, people who come into your life now are people who are here to stay. They can be fun, exciting, charismatic people who want to include you in their lives. They may even want to take you with them on some fascinating little junket, just because they like you. Now is the time to make the most of all your contacts.

When the sun moves into Taurus (April 21–May 20) you are about to discover an eleventh-hour friend who will pull you out of all kinds of unusual scrapes. This person will comfort you emotionally, physically, spiritually, and yes, even financially. What a boon to you, as you do have a tendency to make mischief when things get too dull, as everything must. It usually comes around full circle, so that you alone are left holding the bag. There is, however, one string attached to this eleventh-hour friend. You never get something for nothing, and you may find that when it comes time to pay the piper, the price just may be your freedom. If your eleventh-hour friend turns out to be a Taurus, remember: never, ever toy with his affections. He is called the bull for good reason.

On a happier note, when the sun sees the last days of spring (May 21–June 20), you get lucky, very lucky. If you want to travel, see new places, do unusual things, or experience new lifestyles, then do it. Indulge your fantasies, because you deserve it. Bicycle through China with a Gemini, or an Aquarian friend, or journey to the Kyoto Palace in Japan, just because you have read so much about it. If you want to experience the Orient, you will find that Oriental people will always be lucky for you. If you just want to go on a good local trip, then go to the old seaport of colonial days, Charleston, South Carolina, where you can soak up the atmosphere and culture of the antebellum South. Treat yourself to a stay in one of the old homes that have opened up their doors to weary travelers by offering bed and board.

Since summer is here, when the sun reaches Leo (July 21–August 20) you take out your bathing suit and ask a few of your closest friends to join you at the beach. Friendship is now sweeter and dearer to you than ever. Your friends leave you little time to think, only time to do. I have said it before and will say it again: when looking for a permanent partner, those relationships based on friendship have staying power. So take a good, hard look at those men you call friends, because they will still be around when the others are not.

YOUR COSMIC STAR

Below is a list of the different areas of personal concern and the significance that each plays in your life. How each corresponds to your own personalized Cosmic Star is explained. When the sun passes over each area in turn, that area of your life is highlighted for approximately one month. Knowing this can be very helpful to you when you want to make an important move. This is very valuable information to have when you need to coordinate your best timing with decisive action or start a new project. You know that your cosmic year can easily be individualized. It begins with this year's birthday and ends with your next birthday.

By familiarizing yourself with each astrological area of your Cosmic Star, you will know what part of your life will be paramount and how best to take advantage of your positive qualities.

1. ♎ YOURSELF When the sun highlights Area 1, it accents your need to look and be at your best.

2. ♏ MATERIAL POSSESSIONS When the sun highlights Area 2, you become much more aware of your worth.

3. ♐ ABILITY TO COMMUNICATE When the sun highlights Area 3, you wish to exchange ideas with other people.

4. ♑ HOME AND FAMILY When the sun highlights Area 4, you would like to spend more time at home with your family.

5. ♒ LOVE LIFE When the sun highlights Area 5, what you would really like to do is just enjoy life.

6. ♓ WORK When the sun highlights Area 6, you must work hard for the things you want.

7. ♈ MARRIAGE When the sun highlights Area 7, other people could be ready to make a commitment.

8.   ♋   SUPPORT When the sun highlights Area 8, you may need help.

9.   ♊   TRAVEL When the sun highlights Area 9, you find good luck on the road.

10.   ♋   CAREER When the sun highlights Area 10, career moves can now go public.

11.   ♌   FRIENDS When the sun highlights Area 11, you meet new people and make new friends.

12.   ♍   THE END When the sun highlights Area 12, everything becomes known.

HOW TO USE YOUR COSMIC STAR

The easy-to-use Cosmic Star will help you to personalize your own chart by using your birthday as a starting point. I will begin by showing you where and how your cosmic year begins.

The points of the star move in a counterclockwise direction. Each point represents approximately one month. To make it personally yours, place your birthday at the point marked 1 ♎ . Then, moving down again in a counterclockwise direction, place the next month and your birthday at point 2 ♏, and so forth, placing the same day and the next month at each point until all the points are captioned.

As the year moves along, you can visualize how the sun's transits over these points each month will affect your life. You are now in a better position to anticipate major changes and capitalize on any new opportunities that could present themselves.

If you were born at the end of one sign or at the beginning of another, turn to Appendix A on page 115 to find out exactly what constellation the sun was moving through at the same time of your birth. To check how I individualized my own Cosmic Star, turn to Appendix B on page 125.

Libra

September 21 – October 20

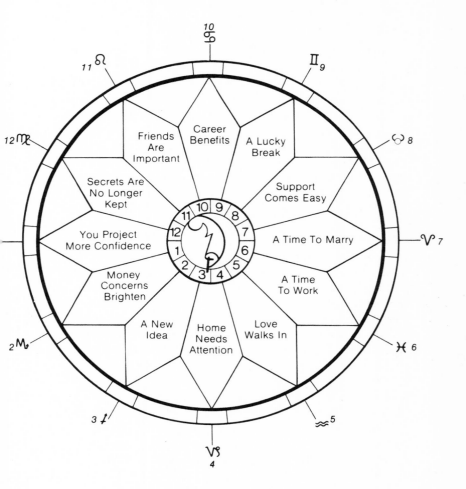

Career Benefits

Friends Are Important

A Lucky Break

Secrets Are No Longer Kept

Support Comes Easy

You Project More Confidence

A Time To Marry

Money Concerns Brighten

A Time To Work

A New Idea

Home Needs Attention

Love Walks In

8

Scorpio

Scorpio women enjoy the reputation of being the most passionate women in the zodiac. I might add that the title is well deserved, but usually well hidden from the stranger's eyes. How utterly fascinating you are! You are a very complex person with many facets to your personality. The sign, Scorpio, is ruled by both the planet Pluto and the planet Mars. You are heir to all the different natures of your symbols: the scorpion, which is rather small in size but is tough and can back up its looks with action; the eagle, which flies high and proud, but misses nothing; the serpent of wisdom, which represents all healers who take on the troubles of the world; and last, the mythical phoenix, which arose out of its own ashes and created life where there was none. At your best, you are the heroines who inspire men to greatness, and at your worst, you are one who keeps your emotions and thoughts to yourself.

What type of man should a Scorpio woman be attracted to? You can't help being attracted to a man who can help you get ahead in the world. When love is involved, many times you have been known to use your head and not your heart. Scorpio women never marry below their socioeconomic level. You may marry at the same level (with the proviso that he is intelligent and ambitious) or you marry up, but never down. You see, when a Scorpio's mother told her, "It's just as easy to love a rich man as a poor man," she listened and believed, just like her sister sign, Capricorn. That is one reason you are financially embarrassed only for the moment, but never really poor.

Very few Scorpio women stray or get a divorce, unless your man has proven himself unworthy of your love by being disloyal and dishonest. Absolute loyalty is a must for you. It is the prize you treasure above anything else, and you want it in any relationship. You can comfort yourself with this thought: a man may leave you, but he will never, ever forget you.

Men find you fascinating because you are cloaked in an aura of mystery and intrigue. That cool, detached presence that you surround yourself with only hints at the secrets that you possess. Some people are put off by this because you appear to be unapproachable. Others are almost mesmerized by your sensuality and your conscious web of secrecy. No one can be noncommittal about a Scorpio woman. You possess a certain charisma that attracts power and powerful people into your circle of friends. Much of your energy (and you have plenty of it) goes into gaining power, especially power over your own destiny. A man does not choose you; you choose him, and you are very discriminating. Once you set your heart on someone or something, you allow your head to take control and then all systems are "go." You aim high. Systematically, you eliminate all obstacles in your way because you see clearly what has to be done and will not rest until you have achieved what you set your sights on.

Intense is a very accurate description of a Scorpio. This is a big plus in the way you play male-female games. That, along with your natural psychic ability, gives you an uncanny way of communicating with anyone you are interested in, without ever a word being spoken. You can intuitively pick up on a man's interest in you, even before he has had a chance to verbalize his intent. It is all part of your overall strategy and approach to life in general. You know you have this ability and you know how to use it.

Scorpio natives are famous for being very interested in unearthing the universal truths, the occult, astrology, and getting to the bottom of any mystery that happens to cross their path. Lots of Scorpios can be found at seminars, demonstrating their use of psychic power, or at classes on astrology and universal timing. If you are a Scorpio interested in basic astrology, you might start a conversation with "What is your sign?" And you really mean it. It is one way to get to the heart of the matter and find out if this person is a suitable companion for you. In other words, one of your mottoes could be "Stay out of the kitchen if you can't stand the heat." Since you are the most passionate women in the zodiac, you need someone who can match you, flame for flame, and take you higher than you ever dreamed of. No wimps need apply! Like Linda Evans's relationship to John Forsyth on *Dynasty,* you need someone who will be your equal, but yet be separate, and most important, someone who will fit into your life's game plan.

During your lifetime, you have probably read hundreds of self-help books or joined classes that helped you to understand yourself better than any other sign. You also learned how to harness the power of self-control and positive suggestion for your benefit. At some time or other, all Scorpios have to learn the secret of patience: everything comes to those who wait.

Your lucky colors are the ones from the dark red family. By wearing the more dominating shades of red, like crimson, maroon, claret, and scarlet, you attract power and the right kind of attention. The best things in life will happen to you when you wear the angry shades of red. If you just happen to find material with silver threads woven through, buy a bolt. The silver threads will offer an extra amount of protection as you go through life. But best of all, it will help you attract incredible wealth and power.

Clothes make the woman. They are an outward symbol that lets society know just what socioeconomic level you are on. In order to be accepted into the stratum of your choice (and believe me, it is your choice), you must dress the part. Fur is definitely "in" for a Scorpio woman. If you can't afford a full-length black mink coat, then perhaps a black cashmere wrap coat with a high silver fox collar will fit the bill. It is very important to give the illusion of wealth. Be sure to keep the fur close to your face, so that it frames your striking features. Evening clothes in daring red and black with silver accents should be set off by high heels and, preferably, black nylons. Last, when you shop for a handbag, buy the most expensive-looking one you can get. Even if you wear jeans, your status will be obvious by your handbag.

Your face should glow with good health, and with a little bit of help from some iridescent makeup. Any one of the metallic colors would bring out the best of your natural features, such as your unusual, catlike eyes. Specifically, try using a dark eye liner and matching mascara to accent the depth of your eyes and to bring out their sparkle. When using eye shadow, do not use the same color as your eyes, because you want people to look at your eyes, not your eye makeup. Your eyes are one of the most expressive parts of your anatomy. You talk with your eyes because for a Scorpio they are the mirrors of the soul. So keep them healthy, and keep them beautiful.

Do not bite your nails! They are your indication of a well psyche. Scorpios have always enjoyed the reputation of being survivors. In the animal kingdom, an animal's nails or claws determine if it will win and live, or lose and die. Your nails should be long enough to do damage but short enough so they won't break off. Make some extra time tonight to give yourself a manicure, and always carry an emery board or a nail file with you, just in case.

Old-timers believed in a lucky touchstone, which they carried in their pockets and handled in times of great stress. They believed it would take worry away, just by fingering it. Today we know better—or do we? Your lucky touchstone is the bloodstone. Handle one when you feel you are losing control. It is believed that within a few minutes you will be able to regain your composure. Other stones that are reputed to confer increased concentration and help a Scorpio focus on the important things are beryl and topaz. Wear them set in silver to ensure no intrusion into your thoughts.

The Scorpio fragrance must speak to him of mystery, long romantic nights, and secret rendezvous. Scents that hint of the mysteries of the universe and shared forbidden passion are good choices for you—perfumes with names like My Sin, Scoundrel, Obsession, Dioressence, and Forever Krystle, which was named for a specific Scorpio lady, Linda Evans, who plays the part of Krystle Carrington on *Dynasty*.

No one else can love as completely as a Scorpio native. You have an insatiable appetite for excitement, love, and romance, so that when the sun enters Pisces (February 21–March 20) you could fall madly, passionately in love. You could find a whole new world opening up for you. You are given many more choices than at any other time of the year, so plan on taking full advantage of this, and shop around. You might spend a few weeks on vacation enjoying the last snows of Aspen. You could take advantage of the skiing, or perhaps try your hand at ice skating or sledding. Later, share some intimate moments with newfound friends in the lounge, or take advantage of some of Aspen's fine restaurants. You can't help but be impressed with the rich and famous you will be in contact with, both on the slopes and at the lodge. It is a time to indulge your senses by doing things you like to do and that interest you. Suggestions: fencing, mystery writing, sailing, or searching for a haunted house. Clearly, the best way to attach your star to one whose star is rising is to find men whose interests mirror your own. It may be worth it to look seriously at the other water signs, another Scorpio or a Pisces or Cancer. (By the way, the Cancer native is a money sign, but he just doesn't seem to talk much about it.)

If you haven't fallen in love yet, in April or May your social life gets a big boost. People who come to you now want to make a commitment to you, or want assurance from you of your loyalty to them. If you decide to opt for a long-term relationship, or to sign a contract, or even get married, now is a time when special relationships get the added insurance that the match will last. If you have made a match with a Taurus, the physical attraction can be incredible. The money won't be too bad, either, but remember: he is very set in his ways and does not enjoy lots of mind games. He can be very stubborn, but then again, so can you!

During June and July, the summer sun beckons you outside to join in having a little fun. It is time to go to the beach, to picnics, and to outdoor celebrations. It is a time for planning, for new places and new faces. This will be a very lucky time for the Scorpio native who wants to take advantage of her natural inclination to explore. The ocean floor will hold some fascination for the Scorpio who is searching for adventure. You may want to indulge your curiosity and take scuba diving classes. One never knows who, or what, one may find down there! An alternative could be an exciting overseas trip due east to Norway, or due south to Rio de Janeiro. Either direction can be the catalyst for some very good fortune to smile on you. You don't want to go underwater and you hate long plane flights? Try a trip to Washington, D.C., or New Orleans—it could net you an invitation to the event of your lifetime. Ann, a Scorpio hostess of the television show *The Hollywood Connection,* can attest to how lucky Washington, D.C., was for her, and it will continue to be so long as she pursues her career from this city. Whatever you do, I know you will enjoy this season with a great passion.

Like your sister sign, Capricorn, you always have been and always will be ambitious. Your public life is one of your most important concerns, and the end of July and the first part of August is a time to go public with any plans you have for ensuring success in your career. You have the energy and support of authority figures to put your plans into action and push for the top. When announcing your plans to the world, do it on a Tuesday for maximum impact.

When summer comes to a close and the sun moves through the constellation Virgo (August 21–September 20), you like gathering your friends around you to share in your joy and good fortune. In many ways you find yourself alone in a crowd. Even if your friends don't quite understand you, they accept you for the person you are, so allow them the privilege of showing you just how much they care.

YOUR COSMIC STAR

Below is a list of the different areas of personal concern and the significance that each plays in your life. How each corresponds to your own personalized Cosmic Star is explained. When the sun passes over each area in turn, that area of your life is highlighted for approximately one month. Knowing this can be very helpful to you when you want to make an important move. This is very valuable information to have when you need to coordinate your best timing with decisive action or start a new project. You know that your cosmic year can easily be individualized. It begins with this year's birthday and ends with your next birthday.

By familiarizing yourself with each astrological area of your Cosmic Star, you will know what part of your life will be paramount and how best to take advantage of your positive qualities.

1. ♏ YOURSELF When the sun highlights Area 1, it accents your need to look and be at your best.

2. ♐ MATERIAL POSSESSIONS When the sun highlights Area 2, you become much more aware of your worth.

3. ♑ ABILITY TO COMMUNICATE When the sun highlights Area 3, you wish to exchange ideas with other people.

4. ♒ HOME AND FAMILY When the sun highlights Area 4, you would like to spend more time at home with your family.

5. ♓ LOVE LIFE When the sun highlights Area 5, what you would really like to do is just enjoy life.

6. ♈ WORK When the sun highlights Area 6, you must work hard for the things you want.

7. ♉ MARRIAGE When the sun highlights Area 7, other people could be ready to make a commitment.

8. ♊ SUPPORT When the sun highlights Area 8, you may need help.

9. ♋ TRAVEL When the sun highlights Area 9, you find good luck on the road.

10. ♌ CAREER When the sun highlights Area 10, career moves can now go public.

11. ♍ FRIENDS When the sun highlights Area 11, you meet new people and make new friends.

12. ♎ THE END When the sun highlights Area 12, everything becomes known.

HOW TO USE YOUR COSMIC STAR

The easy-to-use Cosmic Star will help you to personalize your own chart by using your birthday as a starting point. I will begin by showing you where and how your cosmic year begins.

The points of the star move in a counterclockwise direction. Each point represents approximately one month. To make it personally yours, place your birthday at the point marked 1 ♏ . Then, moving down again in a counter-clockwise direction, place the next month and your birthday at point 2 ♐ , and so forth, placing the same day and the next month at each point until all the points are captioned.

As the year moves along, you can visualize how the sun's transits over these points each month will affect your life. You are now in a better position to

anticipate major changes and capitalize on any new opportunities that could present themselves.

If you were born at the end of one sign or at the beginning of another, turn to Appendix A on page 115 to find out exactly what constellation the sun was moving through at the time of your birth. To check how I individualized my own Cosmic Star, turn to Appendix B on page 125.

Scorpio

October 21 – November 20

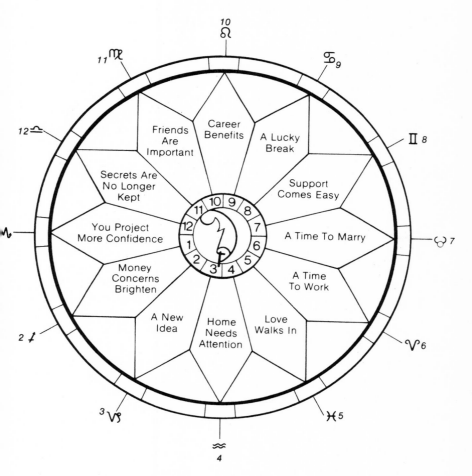

10
♌

11 ♍

♋ 9

12 ♎

♊ 8

Friends Are Important

Career Benefits

A Lucky Break

Secrets Are No Longer Kept

Support Comes Easy

You Project More Confidence

A Time To Marry

♏

☊ 7

Money Concerns Brighten

A Time To Work

2 ♐

A New Idea

Home Needs Attention

Love Walks In

♑ 6

3 ♑

♓ 5

≈
4

Sagittarius

My dear Sagittarius lady, you are the last fire sign in the zodiac. Your watchwords are *action* and *expansion*. You like to do things in a big way (everything you do is big). You are known as the huntress of the sky and can be the most beguiling, exciting, enticing woman when you want to be. Sagittarius's ruler is the planet Jupiter, protector of sportsmen, expander of knowledge, and keeper of the faith. Basically, Jupiter will always provide you with an optimistic outlook that will protect you in hard times and make the good times better.

What attracts a smart girl like you? Wit, brains, fun, games, good looks, and having a fantastic time. When you meet a man, he must appeal to you both physically and intellectually, and he had better be interesting because you don't date just anybody. He must be pretty special for you to even take a second look, and he had better treat you with respect. You have lots of admirers, even after you supposedly settle down, because you are fun to be with and you know how to make people feel special by giving them your full attention. It is not hard to understand, since you are genuinely interested in people. You need lots of freedom of movement; you resist being tied down. In payment for your freedom, you will grant your partner the same privilege. When given your freedom, you are completely trustworthy and trusting. If tied down, you can become a real shrew. Sagittarians don't appear to have a jealous bone in their body. You have structured your life so that you have so many different things going on, you just can't be bothered with wasting time worrying about what someone else is doing. Besides, it is none of your business what he does when he is not with you. He is a big boy and able to take care of himself. "Live and let live" is a rule you live by.

Like other Sagittarius girls, Jane Fonda, who has become a role model for many modern women, has lived her life the way she wanted to live it and in the process has made no concessions and no excuses and has no regrets. Her interests, like yours, are multifaceted and span a wide spectrum. Children and dogs adore you because they know that you like them. You take life and people as you find them, with no hint of imposing your will on others or changing them. You know that things have a way of working themselves out (most of the time in your favor), and you are the eternal optimist.

Sagittarians, unlike most people, have few regrets. You perceive things as they are and accept the way things are done because you have very few illusions about how things should be. You are not out to change the world but to have fun by enjoying life and enjoying the company of all the people you meet along the way.

You sure know how to enjoy yourself and can always be counted on to make a marvelous addition to any party. During your lifetime you will receive thousands of invitations. I suggest that you accept as many as you can. This is one place where the Sagittarian will get much more than her share of the attention. Besides, it is not the actual party you are interested in, but those interesting people you haven't met yet. The more people you meet, the greater your circle of friends, and the greater your circle of friends, the greater your chance of finding Mr. Right. Even if you don't meet him, you will make some fabulous friends and have some wonderful times. No matter what happens, you can't lose now. Who wouldn't go along with that?

Routine has never been one of your strong points, but you really should try to take a little time out each day to spend some time on yourself, meaning your physical self. As a woman gets older, a little time spent taking care of her face will really pay. It takes years off her actual age. You see, your face is what the world sees first and that is how you are remembered. Protest! Protest! You prefer to be seen as natural as possible, showing the world the real you. This is wonderful because you are one of the luckier signs, usually blessed with good skin and enviable bone structure to begin with. Considering all the time you spend outside and how harsh that can be on your skin (wind, cold, sun, and pollution), I would suggest giving your face some extra protection. Afterward, when you finally come inside, just cleanse exposed skin and dab on a little moisturizer. This small intrusion on your valuable time can keep you looking younger and wrinkle-free for many years to come. A Sagittarian girl does not need to go in for flamboyant makeup unless she wants to. However, with all the parties you are invited to, you may want to learn a few techniques for a more glamorous evening look.

Hair, too, is one of the Sagittarian's strong features. Whether you wear your hair short or long, be sure to keep it clean, healthy, and conditioned. If you have long hair, try wearing it in intriguing French braids, or in one long braid down your back, with bits of leather, turquoise beads, or feathers braided in. Anything you wear in your hair will be worth the trouble you had putting it there.

Clothes are another matter. The gravitational pull seems to be to the more casual, go-anywhere styles. You are a lady on the move and you want clothes that will move with you. Many Sagittarians live in jeans and have more than one pair tucked away in their closet. Many of you like to wear them with either a turtleneck sweater or a button-down shirt, with a handmade pullover tied around your neck. For a less casual look, you may want to substitute a tweed or corduroy jacket with leather buttons and suede elbow patches for your usual sweater, and a jeans skirt. All in all, designer Ralph Lauren has your look down to a T. You look the part of a fresh, wholesome country girl. The western styles that remind us of pioneer days were designed with you in mind. Like an all-weather zip-out-lining trench coat, you can go anywhere. The look can take you to any country, ready for anything.

What colors should a Sagittarian wear when she wants to find good luck? They should be rather bright, beginning with royal purple, graduating to woodland violet, and ending with periwinkle blue. Any one of these colors can bring a welcome change in your luck. Now, if you are trying to kindle the flames of love, then add that little hint of fire-engine red or the excitement of raspberry and you will look good enough to eat. Both color combinations will express the excitement that can be generated only by the Sagittarian woman.

Jewelry should be unique and express the real you. Amethyst will blend in beautifully with your lucky colors, but turquoise can ward off evil spirits. Those beautiful American Indian creations you so admire (in silver and turquoise) pull together the country and western look you want—and most Sagittarians can wear big, oversized jewelry. Each design carries with it certain meanings and certain protections and can keep its wearer out of harm's way. Whether you believe it is a talisman or not, it is beautiful jewelry. If it is a one-of-a-kind item, it may not only be a work of art but can also become very valuable.

As you race out the door, going who knows where, perfume may be the last thing on your mind. Think spray cologne for every day and perfume for those extra-special occasions. A number of fragrances that could add a little zing to your life are Ambush, Blue Grass, 4711 eau de cologne, and a men's cologne often worn by women, Canoe.

Your survival kit (and for some of you that means your knapsack) should contain the things that make life easier for you. First, a go-anyplace raincoat; a pad of paper for exchanging names, addresses, and telephone numbers; a pen; a pencil with an eraser; stamps; a comb; and a pair of sunglasses in case you want to go incognito or just want to shade your eyes.

You get a chance to try out those sunglasses right after spring arrives. It becomes a time for love, romance, excitement, and all the kinds of things you thrive on. When the sun crosses the equator (approximately March 21), it brings with it a renewal of life and a second chance for happiness. You, my Sagittarian huntress, are ready and willing to take a chance on love. This can mean anything from joining a survival group out in the wilderness to learning how to ride English style (if you only know how to ride bareback or western style). If, on one of these outings, you just happen to meet an attractive Aries who is looking for a mate, then hang on to him. He is a great lover, and you may just find he is a real soul mate. You two will be equally matched. He will not be the possessive kind, and neither are you. You both need freedom, but there is definitely some kind of physical attraction. This month you will make sparks fly that could ignite a fire that burns a lifetime.

Two months later, as the sun enters Gemini (May 21–June 20), you may find your mind wandering to thoughts of settling down. This will be one of the most important times of the year for you, when new ideas and/or new people come bounding into your life, adding a dimension that can't be seen but sure can be felt. You may begin to think about sharing your life, but on the other hand, you would hate to miss out on anything. You don't have to miss anything. The right person, who can share all the good times as well as the bad, can only enhance your life. If by chance a charming air sign (Gemini, Libra, or Aquarius, but especially a Gemini) comes along, you will both be very pleased to discover that you each know some new, fascinating games to play. You, who have always liked to play teacher, will now have a willing student who loves to learn—but beware—some students can be a handful. You and Gemini, although exact opposites, have quite a lot in common. There is no doubt that there is a definite "meeting of the minds" here, as well as a natural attraction. The best bet for a mutual admiration society would be those signs you have the most in common with. These would be other fire signs: Aries, Leo, or another Sagittarian. Leo can bring you romance and adventure and has the staying power you sometimes lack. Other Sagittarians are fun to be with because you both think along the same lines. An Aries can be just the friend or lover who could entice you with tales of faraway places and interesting people and then take you there.

Do you know who your friends are? Supporters can be found under unusual circumstances and at very odd times. They appear to be the people you have the least in common with and the people you would least expect to help you. These are the cardinal water people, the moon children (Cancer). If they give you their support, they will back you all the way and never let you down.

They are tough in many ways, but please, be sensitive to their feelings. They get hurt awfully easily.

Summer seems to be another time when Lady Luck smiles on you. If you plan a trip, take it between July 21 and August 20, because that is when the positive influences will be in effect. Consider a once-in-a-lifetime trip to the land down under, Australia. (It has been rumored there are more men there than women. True or false, it could be worth checking out.) Or, if you wish to try something a little bit different, rent a villa on the Spanish Riviera. Forgot to renew your passport and can't go out of the country? Then you can always take a trip by horseback down to the Grand Canyon floor and spend a long, quiet night camped out under the stars. Whenever you decide to go, make it a Thursday—this is your lucky day. One thing that Sagittarian women have going for them is their ability to be truly interested in tradition-ally male sports. Capitalize on it—use it. Men love it when you show a genuine interest in their sports and hobbies.

In September or October you get a chance to increase your circle of friends. Don't pass this one up; it is a chance to enrich your total life experience. Most Sagittarians have many friends and acquaintances, but very few best friends. If a Libran or an Aquarian man extends the hand of friendship, take it. Either man can be a great catch. They are both fun, entertaining, and all-around nice guys. In any case, a relationship based on friendship can be very rewarding.

YOUR COSMIC STAR

Below is a list of the different areas of personal concern and the significance that each plays in your life. How each corresponds to your own personalized Cosmic Star is explained. When the sun passes over each area in turn, that area of your life is highlighted for approximately one month. Knowing this can be very helpful to you when you want to make an important move. This is very valuable information to have when you need to coordinate your best timing with decisive action or start a new project. You know that your cosmic year can easily be individualized. It begins with this year's birthday and ends with your next birthday.

By familiarizing yourself with each astrological area of your Cosmic Star, you will know what part of your life will be paramount and how best to take advantage of your positive qualities.

1.   ♐   YOURSELF When the sun highlights Area 1, it accents your need to look and be at your best.

2.   ♑   MATERIAL POSSESSIONS When the sun highlights Area 2, you become much more aware of your worth.

3.   ♒   ABILITY TO COMMUNICATE When the sun highlights Area 3, you wish to exchange ideas with other people.

4.   ♓   HOME AND FAMILY When the sun highlights Area 4, you would like to spend more time at home with your family.

5.   ♈   LOVE LIFE When the sun highlights Area 5, what you would really like to do is just enjoy life.

6.   ♉   WORK When the sun highlights Area 6, you must work hard for the things you want.

7.   ♊   MARRIAGE When the sun highlights Area 7, other people could be ready to make a commitment.

8.   ♋   SUPPORT When the sun highlights Area 8, you may need help.

9.   ♌   TRAVEL When the sun highlights Area 9, you find good luck on the road.

10.   ♍   CAREER When the sun highlights Area 10, career moves can now go public.

11.   ♎   FRIENDS When the sun highlights Area 11, you meet new people and make new friends.

12.   ♏   THE END When the sun highlights Area 12, everything becomes known.

HOW TO USE YOUR COSMIC STAR

The easy-to-use Cosmic Star will help you to personalize your own chart by using your birthday as a starting point. I will begin by showing you where and how your cosmic year begins.

The points of the star move in a counterclockwise direction. Each point represents approximately one month. To make it personally yours, place your birthday at the point marked 1 ♐ . Then, moving down again in a counterclockwise direction, place the next month and your birthday at point 2 ♑, and so forth, placing the same day and the next month at each point until all the points are captioned.

As the year moves along, you can visualize how the sun's transits over these points each month will affect your life. You are now in a better position to

anticipate major changes and capitalize on any new opportunities that could present themselves.

If you were born at the end of one sign or at the beginning of another, turn to Appendix A on page 115, to find out exactly what constellation the sun was moving through at the time of your birth. To check how I individualized my own Cosmic Star, turn to Appendix B on page 125.

Sagittarius

November 21 – December 20

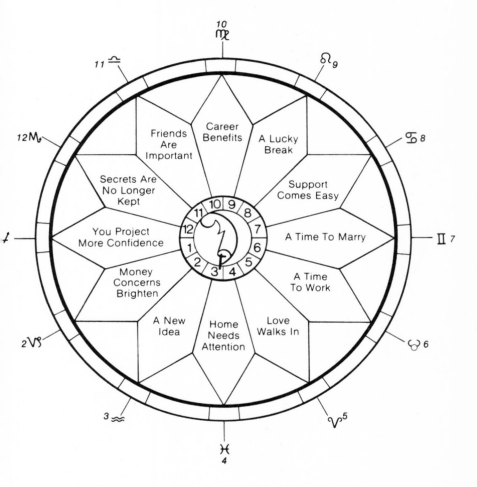

Career Benefits

A Lucky Break

Friends Are Important

Support Comes Easy

Secrets Are No Longer Kept

A Time To Marry

You Project More Confidence

A Time To Work

Money Concerns Brighten

Love Walks In

A New Idea

Home Needs Attention

10

Capricorn

Dear Capricorn: You are the only cardinal earth sign in the zodiac, and many times you will reap the rewards connected with this honorary distinction. You are successful in almost anything you try and can achieve lofty goals if you want to. You are often called a virtual "Wonder Woman" by your peers because you can do almost everything and do it well. Just because you can do it, however, doesn't mean you have to. You should learn to delegate more authority on the job and learn to lighten up a bit at home. Your life will not only be very fulfilling, it will also be long enough to accomplish everything you want to. You see, Capricorn women are known for living to whatever age they choose, so the choice is yours.

Men come in all shapes and sizes, but what interests you the most is their philosophy of life. When a Capricorn woman begins her search for a man, she does her homework first. The man she chooses needs to meet certain preconceived ideals in order to qualify for the final event—a long-term relationship. You take life very seriously and you know that a good relationship must be worked at in order to achieve total satisfaction for both partners. You also know that it will give the greatest return for your efforts.

Capricorn women need men who are nurturers. You need to surround yourself with people who will be supportive of you in any of your endeavors and people who truly love you and really care about your welfare. More then anything else in this world, you need to learn how to relax. A man who can provide you with comfortable surroundings and who can make you smile and even laugh after a long, hard day is a man who can earn your respect. A word of caution, however. He has to be as ambitious as you are, or you will begin to think less of him as time goes on. Once he gets the O.K. from Mom and Dad and your friends and good old Rover, then he will get the O.K. from you. Now that he has passed inspection, and is acceptable to everyone who matters, all systems are "go." You are not a snob, just conscientious. If there is to be a problem, you want to know about it before you get too far into the relationship. One of your mottoes is "Forewarned is forearmed."

(P.S. Most men that you attract have money, power, or both—lucky you!)

You need lots of freedom of movement to wheel and deal on the level that you do. By the way, all Capricorns, both men and women, are wheeler-dealers. You are no stranger to hard work when it comes to getting what you want. You love to work, either in a paying position outside the home, where you can climb the corporate ladder to success, or inside the home, where you are the strategist, directing all the moves and helping your mate and yourself get ahead in the race for the top. Capricorns are definitely the go-getters of this world. You hate to sit still (but you will), because you, like your symbol, the mountain goat, were born to rise above the crowd.

All Capricorn natives are rather conservative. You are not a person who jumps into anything without thinking about it first. In matters of the heart you, like your sister, Scorpio, allow your head to rule your heart, and if you wish it were not so—don't. I know you wish you could just abandon yourself and have fun, but relationships are just too darned important to you. Anyway, you would feel terribly uncomfortable if you didn't look before you leaped. Besides, the relationships you enter into usually last a long time, because yours work when other, less stable relationships fail. You can be very smug because most of your relationships have staying power.

Who wouldn't love to stand out in a crowd and be the center of attention? You certainly would appreciate it. But many times you are very reluctant to blow your own horn. Why? Because of your conservatism. Sometimes you even shun the spotlight because you fear the kind of attention it could generate. You would hate it if you were the butt of someone's joke, or if you were making a fool out of yourself. Many times you will stop just short of taking your rightful place up front because you fear failure. You would rather settle for directing the action from behind the scenes, where you can be much more effective. You *can* have both. One way to do this is specialization. Learn how to capitalize on your natural abilities and skills, so that you have little or no competition in your chosen field. Then be willing to share what you know with others. It will give you more confidence and you will see that people actively seek you out to get the benefit of all your experience and the pleasure of your company. Next time you have a chance to observe Mary Tyler Moore, Dolly Parton, or Eartha Kitt, remember: they are Capricorn natives who have perfected their talents for the enjoyment of others. And you can do the same.

Another way to attract welcome attention is through the clothes you wear. If you are unsure about the look you project or the way you should dress, then read *Dress for Success*, because that is your ultimate goal—you want to succeed. You are what you wear, and clothes do make the woman. Clothes help to inspire confidence in you and your abilities. My first meeting with Susan did exactly that. She gained my confidence immediately because she dressed the part of a successful literary agent and lawyer. You always want to give the impression of professionalism and authority, but not to the exclusion of your femininity. You want a man, once he becomes interested in you, to focus his attention on your face. How can you do this? By drawing his line of vision deliberately up to your face. Either wear a brightly colored shirt or leave your collar open two buttons and then frame it all, like a picture, with a darker suit jacket or sweater. You are deliberately controlling his focus with color.

I know you hate to play games, but the truth is, courtship is a game until you get to know the real person. And until such time, certain rituals must be observed. Most Capricorn women are rather shy and find it extremely difficult to approach or speak to a man first. (You hate to be pushy, but you hate rejection even more.) So if the moment is not to be lost, then you must use every means at your disposal to get him to make the first move—whatever it takes. That means you must make yourself more approachable. Capricorn women do not find it hard to walk into a boardroom full of superiors and hold their own, or to ascend a podium and speak before a multitude of people on a subject dear to their hearts. Walking into an unknown social situation, however, is a very different matter. You may not know what to expect, and you have no way of knowing if you can gain any kind of control over the situation, but you do have control over yourself. *Confidence* is the key word. If you know that you look good and that your clothes are appropriate for the occasion, then hold your head up high, walk proudly, and smile at the man you really want to get to know. You always want to buy quality, the best you can afford—no bargain-basement specials, please! You should include in your wardrobe at least one tailored suit with a matching pair of slacks, a couple of silk blouses, designer jeans, and a top-of-the-line leather handbag and matching briefcase.

You naturally gravitate to the more conservative, authoritative colors on the color wheel. The dark, somber colors of the palette will not only give you more confidence and the upper hand in any situation, they will also encourage good fortune to smile on you. The darker colors speak of sophistication and can travel in any circle: charcoal gray for the boardroom or the office and dove gray for cocktails at the club (of course, if you don't belong to the club, I know you can manage an invitation). Sexy, provocative black attire for the more formal occasions, and match it with black nylons and high-heeled sandals, because "gentlemen prefer legs."

To achieve the total look, you must wear expensive-looking jewelry and gems that catch the eye (but they don't necessarily have to catch the pocketbook). Choose a gem that brings you luck, gives you good fortune, and gives off a small amount of protection, just in case. Look deep into the depths of a sapphire, just as Lady Di did when Bonnie Prince Charles asked her if she would marry him. Your sapphire may not be as big as hers, but it can attract just as much attention. Or contemplate a piece of antique jewelry with fiery garnets, which have adorned dowagers and young women alike. Because you don't buy that much jewelry, I would strongly suggest that you invest in a good-quality piece, and when you wear it you will enjoy it.

If you ask makeup artists what is the most coveted facial feature, they will tell you that it is good bone structure and high cheekbones. All the rest can be covered over or minimized. Well, lucky you! Capricorn natives have wonderful bone structure. Learn how to make the best of what you naturally have and any flaws can be virtually eliminated. You should concentrate on having a conservative, natural daytime look and a bolder, more sultry look for evening. I want to remind you that many business deals, as well as important commitments, are made over dinner. So you want to look healthy and exciting under subdued lighting, not washed-out, pale, or tired.

When it comes to fragrance, I would suggest you find your own signature. You want a fragrance that you can wear all the time and call your own. Once people recognize it, they will associate it with you. Be careful in selecting a scent, because Capricorn's body can sometimes have an adverse reaction to perfume, making the smell different than anticipated. Try L'Aimant, Joy, Enjoli, Charlie, or anything else that strikes your fancy.

I have just given you some ideas on how to use your beauty and sex appeal to get what you want. We already know that you know how to use your brains. So let's put that old saying to rest: "Men don't find smart women appealing." Men find brainy women fascinating, because sexual appeal is mostly in the mind.

Timing is everything! Now, I am going to give you the secret of universal planning, a look into how you can take advantage of your own personal timetable. About the only time we might find you being caught off guard and falling in love is when the sun enters Taurus (May 21–June 20). Practical in almost everything you do, you could now become caught up in a wave of passion, excitement, and emotion. The higher up you go, the less oxygen you get and the more the experience becomes a potentially heady one. Saturday just could be your lucky day. This is also a time you might relax and take time out from your busy schedule to play. Yes, Capricorn, playing is good for you! Let the world see the other side of your personality. Play golf or racquetball at the best club in town. Offer to help with or teach a class in adult education. Or go all out and take a gamble and work for a political party. You will meet a great group of people, and besides, you will be doing something for your country and your fellowman. Playing can have its own rewards.

When the sun enters Cancer (June 21–July 20), half of your solar year is almost over. You could start by getting organized and getting down to some serious looking for a person to share your life with. This could be when you meet Mr. Wonderful. Once an introduction is made, you immediately use your mental checklist and begin taking stock of his family, friends, social position, his compatibility, his goals, what he expects out of life (very important), and then his bank account. My very dear friend Nancy (who happens to be a sister Virgo and one smart lady) once told me that when she meets a man she is serious about, she has an astrological compatibility chart run on him, and if that is satisfactory, she has a credit check run. All in all, not a bad system. Wealth and status turn you on. By the by, a Cancer man has the greatest potential for being a self-made millionaire, so you might want to give him a second glance, and perhaps a third.

Many women today work and I would say that the vast majority of Capricorn women are part of the work force. Capricorn women were liberated long before it became fashionable or popular. Another motto of yours is "It doesn't matter if you are male or female so long as you get the job done." Your career, or that of your consort or mentor, is of the utmost importance. In September or October you stop being concerned about your personal self and begin concentrating on your goals and your public image. It is a time to make your mark. Authority figures are ready to listen. If you don't have a mentor or a career, now is the time when either one of these will miraculously appear. If you are ready to take your rightful place, then go ahead and reach for the brass ring and hold tight. You are it, baby. You are all that you have and you are about to arrive.

Friendships are important to you. You like having someone to share things with, give advice to, and ask opinions of. You have few close friends, and those you usually meet at an organization or a corporation, where everyone is working toward a common goal. In October or November you will learn who your friends really are and who can be counted on. Fifteen years ago (in the month of November) I met my best friend, Julie, at a large corporation in the Washington, D.C., area. Throughout the years, we have traveled different paths, she as an office manager for a famous cartoonist and I as a free-lance writer. Even now, we still find time to enjoy each other's company. Remember: friends you make now last, and you can't do better than friendships in any kind of permanent relationship.

One quick word about Dame Fortune. She lifts up her head to smile at you at summer's end (August through September). If you happen to be in Newport, Rhode Island, Alaska, Brussels, Georgia, or Mexico, her smile is even broader. So be on the lookout this summer—I wouldn't want you to miss her.

YOUR COSMIC STAR

Below is a list of the different areas of personal concern and the significance that each plays in your life. How each corresponds to your own personalized Cosmic Star is explained. When the sun passes over each area in turn, that area of your life is highlighted for approximately one month. Knowing this can be very helpful to you when you want to make an important move. This is very valuable information to have when you need to coordinate your best timing with decisive action or start a new project. You now know that your cosmic year can easily be individualized. It begins with this year's birthday and ends with your next birthday.

By familiarizing yourself with each astrological area of your Cosmic Star, you will know what part of your life will be paramount and how best to take advantage of your positive qualities.

1. ♑ YOURSELF When the sun highlights Area 1, it accents your need to look and be at your best.

2. ♒ MATERIAL POSSESSIONS When the sun highlights Area 2, you become much more aware of your worth.

3. ♓ ABILITY TO COMMUNICATE When the sun highlights Area 3, you wish to exchange ideas with other people.

4. ♈ HOME AND FAMILY When the sun highlights Area 4, you would like to spend more time at home with your family.

5. ♌ LOVE LIFE When the sun highlights Area 5, what you would really like to do is just enjoy life.

6. ♊ WORK When the sun highlights Area 6, you must work hard for the things you want.

7. ♋ MARRIAGE When the sun highlights Area 7, other people could be ready to make a commitment.

8.   ♌   SUPPORT When the sun highlights Area 8, you may need help.

9.   ♍   TRAVEL When the sun highlights Area 9, you find good luck on the road.

10.   ♎   CAREER When the sun highlights Area 10, career moves can now go public.

11.   ♏   FRIENDS When the sun highlights Area 11, you meet new people and make new friends.

12.   ♐   THE END When the sun highlights Area 12, everything becomes known.

HOW TO USE YOUR COSMIC STAR

The easy-to-use Cosmic Star will help you to personalize your own chart by using your birthday as a starting point. I will begin by showing you where and how your cosmic year begins.

The points of the star move in a counterclockwise direction. Each point represents approximately one month. To make it personally yours, place your birthday at the point marked 1♑ . Then, moving down again in a counterclockwise direction, place the next month and your birthday at point 2 ♒, and so forth, placing the same day and the next month at each point until all the points are captioned.

As the year moves along, you can visualize how the sun's transits over these points each month will affect your life. You are now in a better position to anticipate major changes and capitalize on any new opportunities that could present themselves.

If you were born at the end of one sign or at the beginning of another, turn to Appendix A on page 115, to find out exactly what constellation the sun was moving through at the time of your birth. To check how I individualized my own Cosmic Star, turn to Appendix B on page 125.

Capricorn

December 21 – January 20

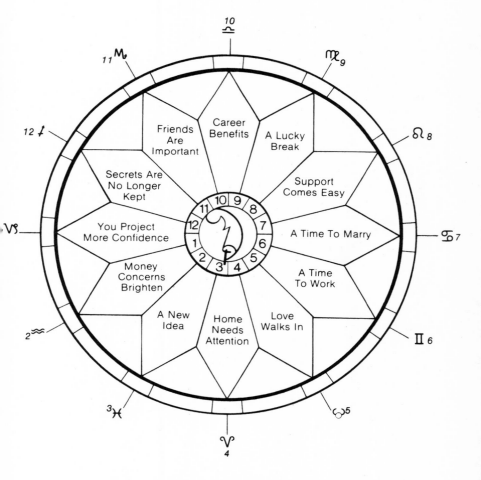

- Career Benefits
- Friends Are Important
- A Lucky Break
- Secrets Are No Longer Kept
- Support Comes Easy
- You Project More Confidence
- A Time To Marry
- Money Concerns Brighten
- A Time To Work
- A New Idea
- Home Needs Attention
- Love Walks In

11

Aquarius

In ancient Egypt, the priests learned from the stars how to predict, with great accuracy, the welcome rising of the Nile River. It was believed that the coming of the Aquarian sun (symbolized by the water bearer) would bring with it the floods that meant life for the Egyptian people. Children born in that month were believed to be born with the gift of second sight, or prophecy. That is one reason that the constellation of Aquarius is designated as the protective sign of the astrologer.

Aquarians have earned the nickname of "gregarious Aquarius" because they are fun-loving and unpredictable. You are ruled by the planet Uranus and are probably one of the most misunderstood signs in the zodiac. It has been noted by actress and astrologer Arlene Dahl that "You are a loner who hates to be alone." You just naturally hear a different drummer than the rest of us and march to a different beat. You don't really care, since you truly like to be different. Sometimes I think you like to shock your family and friends just to get their reaction. Unlike most people in this world, who are trying to figure out how we are all alike, you are trying to figure out how we are different. That is why you have so many friends, because you appreciate their individuality and you treasure their uniqueness. You are that rare, undemanding friend who can accept people as they are and have no intention of trying to change them or make them into something they are not. Yet you hate it when others try to change you or your point of view, because you usually know what is right and what is wrong for you. You are a big girl now, with the intelligence of a genius, who can sift through all the nonsense and get right to the heart of the matter. Once you know what is true, you can make up your own mind and then follow through.

Is Aquarius looking for a man? Probably not, because you are really looking for a friend. The men that you want to attract are men who are interested in playing a few games and sharing some interesting ideas. You need the stimulation and the challenge of a new situation and you, like your Gemini sister, get bored rather quickly. You are also a very distracting influence and always seem to surround yourself with fun and excitement. That, in turn, attracts very good-looking, exciting males, who are out to show you a good time. One slight problem you might run into could prove to be rather sticky. Beware of the man who shows the least bit of jealousy toward you, your friends, or your past loves. You have the habit of attracting men who are used to being in the limelight. Trouble could brew if you manage to steal the show. You don't mean to, but you are just so vivacious and charismatic that you can't help yourself. Basically, it seems that the majority of men you have loved and who have loved you usually want to remain on friendly terms with you, even after the affair is over. It seems that the important relationships are never really over—they just evolve into something more comfortable and compatible with your lifestyle.

Aquarians appear to be the magicians of the zodiac. You make everything seem easier than it is. In reality, it is all an illusion. You also tend to make friends easily and are one who truly enjoys socializing. You never let class or a person's socioeconomic level obscure the more important point—that people are people no matter where you go. Numbered among your many talents and abilities are your social skills. The best skill you possess is your ability to make the person you are with feel comfortable. You draw him out with your exchange of unusual ideas and make him feel he is the most important person in the world. You meet and know so many people that some Aquarians confess to being able to recognize a face but not a name. If you have ever been totally embarrassed because of this, there are two ways of handling it. One: take a course in increasing your memory capacity and maybe you can meet some very interesting men who will remember your name, or whose names you can't forget. Two: you might go up to someone you think you recognize and begin a conversation with "Don't I know you? Aren't you so-and-so, the famous author?" He will be flattered that you thought he was famous, and if you know him, he will refresh your memory. If you don't know him, you soon will! Believe me, either way he won't forget you.

Frankly, you adore men and, I might add, the feeling is mutual. Just because you enjoy male companionship doesn't mean you are willing to give up any of your girlfriends for one big "maybe." A Saturday night (Saturday being one of your luckier days) out with the girls, or one special girlfriend, can be just as much fun as a night out on the town with the boys. You can talk girl-talk, get caught up on the latest gossip, or just flirt outrageously with the hired help, and besides, maybe your friend has a brother, uncle, or kissing cousin you haven't met before. Think of it—isn't it nice not to be tied down to one man? This way, all kinds of new men can appreciate you. In any event, you are less likely to get into trouble when you and your girlfriend are a twosome and you stick together than if you went out alone. Many an Aquarian's reputation precedes her. Aquarians are famous for trying anything once. Admit it: lots of times you make mischief on a whim, just to see the effect. Never, ever mean or curt, when you do make mischief it is usually for a specific purpose. In the case of Helen Gurley Brown, it is to raise the consciousness of women, and in the case of Gypsy Rose Lee, it was to entertain. Both Aquarians, and both became famous for what they did best.

It is a very good thing that Lady Luck is always at your elbow, tagging along to keep you out of harm's way. Lucky you, in more ways than one. After a short while, when you have time to think things out, you may begin to worry about all of the "might have beens." Well, it is all over, so don't fret. Try to relax, take a nice hot bath, and have a warm glass of milk before you snuggle down in bed with the latest best-seller. Then see how quickly you drift off. Uranus just happens to rule tomorrow, so it will be just as exciting as today, because you wouldn't have it any other way.

Clothes are an entirely different matter. Basically, you enjoy and appreciate nice clothes. However, some of your clothes are a little offbeat; they reflect who you are, where you are going, and what your philosophy of life is. You can be a kaleidoscope of different colors, ideas, and interests. The Aquarian native is naturally curious about everything and everyone she comes in contact with. Sometimes you use clothes as a way of trying on other people's personality and culture. You are just dying to try it out, to see how it all fits and if it suits you. One moment you can play "dress up," next moment beach bum, and then change the look completely by donning a three-piece suit and carrying a briefcase. I would suggest you have one of everything, so you can be what you want to be whenever the mood strikes you. Too expensive? Well, a suitable wardrobe should reflect your taste and include one long skirt and one silk blouse for formal wear. You should have one matching suit to take you wherever you want to go and one Hawaiian shirt and cutoffs for casual wear. I might add that most of all you love role-playing, and clothes help in defining the roles you play. Aquarians can make money (lots of it) in television, radio, or the movies. Marcia, a beautiful Aquarian technical director at one of the country's newest television stations, could tell you all about the lucky breaks she has experienced in television communications. Her star is still on the rise and will remain so, as long as she wants to stay in the field. I hope it will be a long time.

Color—you love lots of color. One very fortunate color for you is electric blue. Others are cobalt, indigo, royal, and azure blue. These colors will surely get you noticed, but beyond that, their vibrations draw to you the same kind of intense experiences that the colors suggest. Combine these with either a multicolored print or colorful stripes and wow! What a look! Alternatively, you could combine the blue you have chosen with a stark or creamy white. Not only will it be lucky for you, it could also prove financially beneficial. You can't help but notice that the nicest things will happen to you when you wear blue or white, or both colors together.

Now you should think about makeup. Yes, you hate routine, because there are a lot more interesting things to do than wash your face, apply your makeup, and keep it fresh all day. Granted, you would rather be doing other things, but you always want to look your best. For formal occasions, make the extra effort. Go all out—wear eye shadow to call attention to your beautiful eyes and stardust on bare shoulders to call attention there. For everyday wear, when you just want to be naturally beautiful, add a light touch of blusher to your cheeks, a dab of color on your lips, and just a hint of color around your eyes. Be sure to moisturize, moisturize, moisturize. Basically, you have beautiful skin, but as you get older your skin could give away your age. What you used to take for granted could be lost to you forever. Makeup is important and highly visible, but an even more important ritual, besides moisturizing your skin, is the care you give your teeth. See your dentist regularly and be sure to brush after every meal. Carrying a toothbrush and toothpaste in your purse may make all the difference in the world as to whether you are asked to stay over or are asked to come back again for an encore.

Magic can be found in an ancient fossil called amber, which is often come upon by the sea. This link with the past brings a sense of what went before and the luck of longevity. Wear it in good health and let its vibrations protect you against the worries and sins of the past. There are two pieces of jewelry that should be a must for you. One is an intriguing initial ring that you design and make yourself in a jewelry design class, and the other is an ankle bracelet, which will call attention to your trim ankles and afford you a certain amount of protection as well. Long ago, ankle bracelets were believed to be talismans that would keep their owner prepared and alert at all times.

You look wonderful, you are up on the latest, you have a good measure of protection, and now all you need is the missing ingredient—fragrance. Most Aquarians are very sensitive to cheap, synthetic scents. Buy colognes or perfumes that appeal to your senses first; then use the same scent or fragrance for your body powder, bath products, and hand cream. You might like to try Ciera, Norell, Jontue, or Enjoli Midnight.

The majority of Aquarians were born with a special gift for perfect timing. In other words, you are usually in the right place at the right time. But you sure could use a datebook or calendar to record and remember the who, what, where, how, and why! When May and June roll around, you should plan on even more good times. Take advantage of the late spring weather and diminished crowds by taking some extra time off. Spring in New England can be especially rewarding if you plan on spending a few days in Massachusetts to visit Cape Cod, or take a leisurely stroll down the streets of Boston. You may wish to travel in the opposite direction, to the state of Arizona. A vacation in the right location could yield a big profit for you this year. This is definitely a time when you will have more than your share of charisma and you just naturally seem to attract lots of the good things that life has to offer.

Fun comes to an end and the more serious side of love could spill over into July and August, when you become the object of someone's affection. People who are about to have a strong influence on you are about to come into your life. These same people are ready to make the commitment to stay there for a while. When choosing an important relationship, look very hard for the people who put out a strong Gemini or Libran vibration. A Leo man could be rather captivating. Not only is he one of the best-looking men in the zodiac, but his aura also attracts people of wealth, substance, and culture. Phrased a different way, he can open new doors for you.

When the sun begins its journey south in September, you get itchy feet. You are ready for anything, and foreign travel could be just the lucky break you have been looking for. No do-it-yourself vacations for you! Go to a reputable travel agency (by the way, travel agents are very lucky for you) and tell them you want to visit exciting places, like Peru, to see the sunset at Machu Picchu, or New Zealand. These two countries and Sweden are places and have people who will always be fortunate for you.

When the sun enters Sagittarius, we begin the ritual of celebration. The holidays are a time to appreciate the friends in your life. You have all kinds of friends: the Sagittarian friend who is always asking you out; the Aries friend who is so dependable; the Virgo friend who is willing to give his heart and his support to you. These, and more, are the people in your life who love you, care about you, and wish you well.

YOUR COSMIC STAR

Below is a list of the different areas of personal concern and the significance that each plays in your life. How each corresponds to your own personalized Cosmic Star is explained. When the sun passes over each area in turn, that area of your life is highlighted for approximately one month. Knowing this can be very helpful to you when you want to make an important move. This is very valuable information to have when you need to coordinate your best timing with decisive action or start a new project. You know that your cosmic year can easily be individualized. It begins with this year's birthday and ends with your next birthday.

By familiarizing yourself with each astrological area of your Cosmic Star, you will know what part of your life will be paramount and how best to take advantage of your positive qualities.

1. ♒ **YOURSELF** When the sun highlights Area 1, it accents your need to look and be at your best.

2. ♓ **MATERIAL POSSESSIONS** When the sun highlights Area 2, you become much more aware of your worth.

3. ♈ **ABILITY TO COMMUNICATE** When the sun highlights Area 3, you wish to exchange ideas with other people.

4. ♋ **HOME AND FAMILY** When the sun highlights Area 4, you would like to spend more time at home with your family.

5. ♊ **LOVE LIFE** When the sun highlights Area 5, what you would really like to do is just enjoy life.

6. ♌ **WORK** When the sun highlights Area 6, you must work hard for the things you want.

7. ♌ **MARRIAGE** When the sun highlights Area 7, other people could be ready to make a commitment.

8. ♍ **SUPPORT** When the sun highlights Area 8, you may need help.

9. ♎ **TRAVEL** When the sun highlights Area 9, you find good luck on the road.

10. ♏ **CAREER** When the sun highlights Area 10, career moves can now go public.

11. ♐ **FRIENDS** When the sun highlights Area 11, you meet new people and make new friends.

12. ♑ **THE END** When the sun highlights Area 12, everything becomes known.

HOW TO USE YOUR COSMIC STAR

The easy-to-use Cosmic Star will help you to personalize your own chart by using your birthday as a starting point. I will begin by showing you where and how your cosmic year begins.

The points of the star move in a counterclockwise direction. Each point represents approximately one month. To make it personally yours, place your birthday at the point marked 1 ≈ . Then, moving down again in a counterclockwise direction, place the next month and your birthday at point 2 ⊁ , and so forth, placing the same day and the next month at each point until all the points are captioned.

As the year moves along, you can visualize how the sun's transits over these points each month will affect your life. You are now in a better position to anticipate major changes and capitalize on any new opportunities that could present themselves.

If you were born at the end of one sign or at the beginning of another, turn to Appendix A on page 115 to find out exactly what constellation the sun was moving through at the time of your birth. To check how I individualized my own Cosmic Star, turn to Appendix B on page 125.

Aquarius

January 21 – February 20

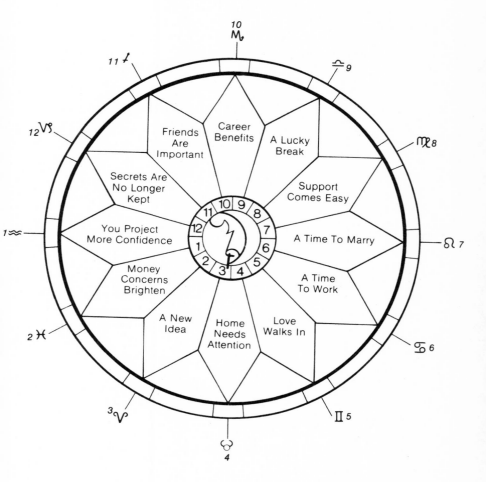

 *Pisces*

The best is always saved until last. In this case, the Pisces native is one of the best, and the very last sign in the zodiac. As a Piscean, you are ruled by the mystical planet Neptune, and the symbol of your sign is mighty Neptune's trident. The god Neptune used his trident to calm the angry seas and keep order among the creatures that dwelled there. You, like Neptune, have power, but it tends to remain beneath the surface, unseen by most people, because they don't know what to look for. Just because something can't be seen doesn't mean that it doesn't exist. We can only see its results. For good or evil, you definitely have power. The "Pisces look" is a rather unusual, delicate look, and the people who see you think of you as being rather frail and ultrafeminine. What they don't seem to understand is that although you appear fragile, it is all an illusion and you are an enigma. People see in you what they want to see, and that appears to be fine with you, so long as it does not hurt anyone. Some men will want to fantasize that you are a damsel in distress and only they can rescue you. Allow them that gentlemanly pleasure. Some men's fancy will be caught immediately and they will probably want to see if you are a dream that might fade in the evening or if you are real (which, of course, you are, but keep them guessing until sunrise, when you have their undivided attention).

Fortunately, you do have the capacity for incredible, creative brilliance, along with an inexhaustible inner strength that will allow you to do anything you want to do. It appears to come from a source that you can draw on at any time, yet it seems to come out of nowhere. It gives you the ability to create your own destiny and lets you cope with and overcome almost any situation that could possibly arise.

The Pisces woman is a special kind of lady who doesn't really need to look for a man—he looks for you. The man who finds you must be a nurturer who is willing to support you and your many talents one hundred percent. He cannot, or should not, be insecure or self-serving. Be very careful, because if he tries to use or abuse you or your talents for his own personal gain, he will only be instrumental in bringing about his own destruction. A Pisces woman needs a man who is of the "one-woman" variety, because you are known as a one-man woman. If you are provoked, you can become rather possessive and jealous, especially where love is concerned. Basically, however, you attract not only the honorable type, but also the doers and pragmatists of the zodiac. Remember: the people you attract can be very critical and hard on themselves, so turn on that charm, be sympathetic and understanding, and most of all, be kind. He can be a dear man, who helps you to get the things you want done by organizing it, so that you can make things happen. With all your talents, he can make all your dreams come true. Teamwork is the real key. You can handle the creative aspects (Pisces has the reputation for being the creative genius of the zodiac), and he can handle the business end, along with any of those mundane little details that you really hate to be bothered with. It isn't that you are afraid of hard work (you will do it if you have to), but you hate to bother with minor details. Keep an eye out for the man who can supply you with the qualities you lack, and vice versa.

All Pisces love to be in love and could be a target for a good sob story. People may try to pull the wool over your eyes, but somehow you never really get taken in. It is very hard to lie blatantly to a Pisces native. There appears to be a guardian angel always watching out for you. Somehow men and women just naturally are very protective of you and are ready to look out for your best interests. You have a sweet-tempered, gentle disposition that endears you to the people you meet. But when you fall in love, you should try to be very discriminating. A word of caution—be discreet. You could, at some time, find yourself in the role of the other woman. Do not protest. As one of your sisters once said on the subject, "We love whom we love. Sometimes we have no choice in the matter."

It also must be mentioned at this time that many of your present relationships are karmic in nature. If love was true, then maybe pure love is strong enough to bridge the gap between time and dimension. Who is to say that love dies? Most Pisceans like to believe it goes on forever. Admit it. You are fascinated by all the possibilities of things that can't be seen but whose influence can be felt. Considered by others to have a sixth sense, you are one of the most sensitive, psychic signs in astrology. It is believed you have the ability to direct this intuitive power for whatever purpose you choose. Most of you tend to use this gift to keep out of harm's way and to protect yourself, your psyche, your loved ones, and even perfect strangers if you deem it necessary. Some Pisceans take up the study of the spiritual side of life—like parapsychology, ghost hunting, life beyond death, and other mysteries of the universe that have no answers at the present time. Maybe you and those like you will find some of the answers, but until then, many people will still believe you could be bewitched, or perhaps just plain bewitching. Whichever it is, you enjoy the reputation of being beguiling.

You hate to spend a lot of time at any one thing, and therefore you like to give expression to each of your talents. You also like to freshen up your residence, your friends, your job, your men, and maybe even your entire wardrobe every once in a while. As the other part of your duality, you hate to throw anything out, just in case it comes back into style. Possibly, when it does go out of style you can resume wearing it because it will now set you apart as an individual. Besides, although you crave change, you also know how to surround yourself with comfort, by keeping things that are familiar to you close at hand. You also have great taste and know which old favorites make you feel good. When you feel good, you look terrific in a very subtle but sexy way.

Pisces women can be very fond of clothes, like designer Gloria Vanderbilt and actress Elizabeth Taylor. Your clothes should mirror a certain image of long ago. Let them speak of romance and a softer, feminine look than is popular today with most women. Draw on the past by choosing styles from the days of chivalry or the age of Queen Victoria. Perhaps you might try a look that suggests the excitement and adventure of the 1920s: flappers, bathtub gin, Hollywood, when everyone lived in the grand manner and anyone could be a star. All of this can be achieved with innocent little prints and soft materials that drape beautifully when made into a dress. Set the mood with perfumed candlelight and records of torch songs. Embody the spirit of the past to reclaim your future. Pat is a wonderful example of a modern-day Pisces. Even though she is an executive for the Department of Agriculture, she knows how to dress for success without losing any of her old-world charm. Everything is always soft, feminine, pretty, and up to date. For instance, once she wore a top of the softest powder pink, with a matching pink, beige, and taupe plaid skirt. She completed the look with a unique natural silk jacket that was great for business. But remove the jacket and she could be ready to play after dark. Wow! What a woman!

Clothes get the attention, but color draws the luck. As for color and lighting —think moonlight and all those colors connected with it, because they create the aura. All shades of white are the ones to wrap yourself in for luck and/or protection. From stark white to the light hues called "candlelight," "moonglow," and "lightning"—these are the colors that not only can be worn year-round, but can also draw to you what you want. Again, the choice is yours. Add to this a touch of sea-foam green, silver, or lavender and you can be lucky in love, along with everything else. A word of warning: never wear dark, depressing colors. Choose colors to match your "up" moods, or ones that will give you a little lift when you need to get through a hard day.

Makeup is usually fun for you and you love to pamper yourself with its luxury. If you don't do so already, treat yourself to the works at your favorite beauty salon every few months, just because you deserve it. A manicure, a pedicure (take good care of your feet, since Pisces rules feet, and they will take good care of you), a facial, and a lesson from a master makeup artist should do it. Again, you want that soft, natural, romantic look. Pay particular attention to your eyes, and get yourself a good haircut if you need a trim. Lots of Pisceans of all ages are known to be sensitive to synthetic products, so you might want to try some of the natural or herbal products that can now be found in health food and specialty stores. Make bathtime a time to relax, contemplate your day, or just pamper yourself with body lotions, bath oils, perfumed soaps, and fragrant powders. When applying lotion, apply it all over your body, including your feet. This will give you a velvety, touchable skin that not only looks good but smells good, too. Be careful when you mix fragrances. They should harmonize or at least blend in with one another. A few suggestions: Jungle Gardenia, Sculptura, Tabu, Chanel No. 19, or Chantilly, and you might even try Vanderbilt.

Dame Fortune will smile favorably on you every time you wear jewelry made of ivory. There are different kinds of ivory—from little, carved figurines and beads to intricate pieces of scrimshaw. Scrimshaw is especially appropriate. It was an art form practiced by the men who went to sea in the old wooden whalers. They had lots of time on their hands as they waited for a sighting. They would carve, or whittle, small household items, like buttons, corset stays, crochet hooks, and pie crimpers, from the teeth and bones of whales. For themselves they made talismans, to protect them in the coming hunt, and many pieces still can be found in New England or Hawaii. Old scrimshaw tends to be expensive but it is available, along with many new pieces. Every lady should also have her own string of pearls, which are believed to be your personal protector of health. Pearls with a pink hue will always add luster to your skin.

Every Pisces native has the ability to tune into her own special timing, if you just get in touch with yourself. Your birthday month will be the best time for making any necessary changes. You need time to adjust to all the things you learned about yourself last year. This year is going to be better than last year.

When the sun moves into Cancer (June 21–July 20) you may be ready to follow your heart's desire. Summer is the best time to spend at the beach, and that is one place where you can be very happy. Rent a house on the Maine coast with a few close friends (preferably your water friends, Cancer, Scorpio, or another Pisces). Spend moonlit evenings partying until dawn and long, lazy days walking on the beach. Or spend some time enjoying Vermont's lakes, ponds, and rivers and commune with Nature. If you invite your friends along to share this time with you, another Pisces will respect you and will not intrude on your privacy. If you take a Cancer friend, he or she will attract and invite all kinds of people over for dinner and good "down home" conversation (Cancers are great cooks and can't resist the chance to feed some poor hungry stranger). A Scorpio friend always attracts the unusual, as well as some of the most fascinating people you will ever meet. All of these friends can't wait to introduce you to their other friends. But all three signs will respect your feelings and your privacy if that is what you want.

The months of August and September bring about some marvelous opportunities. Things open up for you and you now are in great demand. People seek you out to create a one-on-one relationship. This is a time when a man could come along and make all your dreams come true. He may not be as sensitive as you, but if he is of the earth elements (Virgo, Capricorn, or Taurus), he has the strength and courage to help you realize all your dreams and stay with you even when the going gets rough. If he makes you an offer you can't refuse, then don't. This could be the right one.

In October or November, your urge to travel may not be put off any longer. If this is the year to go abroad, first take a language class in Spanish or Portuguese and then make your plans. Portugal is considered the bargain of the century, and its people will always bring you lots of luck. (Leave on a Thursday to increase your luck.) Or, from Portugal, take the train to Seville, Spain, and see what Lady Luck has in store for you there. Besides, a response of "Yo no hablo español" might be just the bait needed to meet a tall, dark, handsome man.

As the sun moves through Capricorn, it is time to renew old acquaintances and make new ones. This is a season to give thanks and enjoy the close friendships you have made. You have a few close friends, but friends are treated like family because you love and cherish them. It is also a time to make the most of all the parties you will be invited to, and if a Capricorn asks you out—go! Capricorn men not only make wonderful, dependable friends, but they can be very persuasive and kind of sexy, in a good-looking, boyish way. Kathy and Steve are a classic example of a working Pisces and Capricorn relationship. They and their two children, Jason and Heath, make a most beautiful family that works toward a common goal. I think that Kathy and

Steve work very well together and really enjoy each other's company when given those rare moments alone. Again, Capricorn friends can make Pisces dreams come true—whatever they may be.

YOUR COSMIC STAR

Below is a list of the different areas of personal concern and the significance that each plays in your life. How each corresponds to your own personalized Cosmic Star is explained. When the sun passes over each area in turn, that area of your life is highlighted for approximately one month. Knowing this can be very helpful to you when you want to make an important move. This is very valuable information to have when you need to coordinate your best timing with decisive action or start a new project. You know that your cosmic year can easily be individualized. It begins with this year's birthday and ends with your next birthday.

By familiarizing yourself with each astrological area of your Cosmic Star, you will know what part of your life will be paramount and how best to take advantage of your positive qualities.

1. ♓ YOURSELF When the sun highlights Area 1, it accents your need to look and be at your best.

2. ♈ MATERIAL POSSESSIONS When the sun highlights Area 2, you become much more aware of your worth.

3. ♉ ABILITY TO COMMUNICATE When the sun highlights Area 3, you wish to exchange ideas with other people.

4. ♊ HOME AND FAMILY When the sun highlights Area 4, you would like to spend more time at home with your family.

5. ♋ LOVE LIFE When the sun highlights Area 5, what you would really like to do is just enjoy life.

6. ♌ WORK When the sun highlights Area 6, you must work hard for the things you want.

7. ♍ MARRIAGE When the sun highlights Area 7, other people could be ready to make a commitment.

8. ♎ SUPPORT When the sun highlights Area 8, you may need help.

9. ♏ TRAVEL When the sun highlights Area 9, you find good luck on the road.

10. ♐ CAREER When the sun highlights Area 10, career moves can now go public.

11. ♑ FRIENDS When the sun highlights Area 11, you meet new people and make new friends.

12. ♒ THE END When the sun highlights Area 12, everything becomes known.

HOW TO USE YOUR COSMIC STAR

The easy-to-use Cosmic Star will help you to personalize your own chart by using your birthday as a starting point. I will begin by showing you where and how your cosmic year begins.

The points of the star move in a counterclockwise direction. Each point represents approximately one month. To make it personally yours, place your birthday at the point marked 1 ♓ . Then, moving down again in a counterclockwise direction, place the next month and your birthday at point 2 ♈, and so forth, placing the same day and the next month at each point, until all the points are captioned.

As the year moves along, you can visualize how the sun's transits over these points each month will affect your life. You are now in a better position to anticipate major changes and capitalize on any new opportunities that could present themselves.

If you were born at the end of one sign or at the beginning of another, turn to Appendix A on page 115 to find out exactly what constellation the sun was moving through at the time of your birth. To check how I individualized my own Cosmic Star, turn to Appendix B on page 125.

Pisces

February 21 – March 20

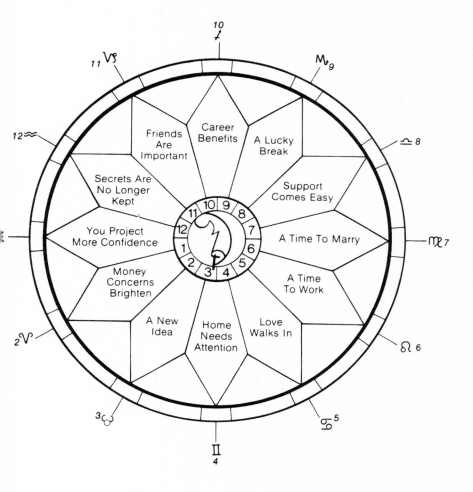

- 10 ♐
- 11 ♑
- 12 ♒
- 9 ♏
- 8 ♎
- 7 ♍
- 6 ♌
- 5 ♋
- 4 ♊
- 3 ♉
- 2 ♈

Career Benefits

Friends Are Important

A Lucky Break

Secrets Are No Longer Kept

Support Comes Easy

You Project More Confidence

A Time To Marry

Money Concerns Brighten

A Time To Work

A New Idea

Home Needs Attention

Love Walks In

13

Astrological Sun Sign Combinations

This chapter is here because everyone wants to know how they will relate to other people and other people's sun signs. We are naturally curious to see what other people's goals and philosophy of life are and if they can harmonize with our own.

Sun signs are very important. They give us a natural starting point in figuring out where a relationship is going. Remember, though, that each person is a unique individual and each relationship has its own personality. So if you want more specifics, you must have a full personal chart and a comparison chart done by a reputable astrologer. From them you can learn the different strengths and weaknesses that could develop in the relationship. My suggestion to anyone who is interested in entering into a relationship is always "Trust your gut instinct and go with it." Keep in mind that all relationships, no matter how good, will come under cosmic stress eventually and will have to be worked at. Both parties will also eventually have to effect a compromise. In a time of crisis, cool heads must prevail in order for the relationship to survive.

The sun sign combinations below are used as examples of what can hold and sustain a relationship in certain stressful situations. When looking for positive elements to focus on, try concentrating on open and honest communication. As you know, it takes two separate personalities to make a relationship. No one combination is better or worse than another. Every relationship has a chance to work and work well, or a chance not to work at all.

Aries and Aries
The right chemistry is definitely there. Life certainly will never be boring, because you will challenge each other to go on to be the best you could possibly be.

Aries and Taurus
Fast and sensuous, that is the only way to describe this relationship. Aries is fast and knows how to draw Taurus out, and Taurus knows moves that will surprise and delight the Aries native.

Aries and Gemini
This relationship may start on a flirtatious note, but could end up on a more permanent one.

Aries and Cancer
Cancer has the knack of knowing just what Aries needs, and Aries knows how to comfort and protect Cancer.

Aries and Leo
An immediate attraction occurs. This could be the great love of your life and it could go on forever, if that is what you want.

Aries and Virgo
Your approach to life is entirely different, but Aries can fulfill Virgo's every fantasy and Virgo can make life oh so comfortable for Aries.

Aries and Libra
In this case, opposites attract. You each have a special gift to bring to the relationship. You each have what the other lacks.

Aries and Scorpio
There are definitely fireworks in this one. Mars, the planet that rules sexual attraction, rules both Aries and Scorpio, and that gives you both the stamina to be equals.

Aries and Sagittarius
One very lucky combination. Sagittarius wants to play teacher to Aries' eager student. This could equal some pretty interesting classes, or homework.

Aries and Capricorn
Curiously, this relationship can work, but not without a few compromises. Aries can create a wonderful private life for Capricorn, and Capricorn can help Aries achieve a comfortable public life.

Aries and Aquarius
You are marvelous together. Aries is sheer energy and Aquarius is sudden change. Therefore, there will never be a dull moment in this relationship.

Aries and Pisces
Pisces intuitively knows what buttons to push to turn Aries on. Aries will surround Pisces with an exciting life that Pisces could really get into.

Taurus and Taurus
You share, along with your love, many of the same endearing traits, and this in itself will contribute to holding the relationship together, even during difficult times.

Taurus and Gemini
A learning experience for both of you. Taurus—the Gemini native can teach you much about life; and you, Gemini, have much to teach Taurus about finishing what they start.

Taurus and Cancer
What a marvelous combination. Not only can you be friends, but lovers as well, and best of all, because you are both money signs, you can have double the money.

Taurus and Leo
The magic is definitely there. Taurus loves to be included in Leo's exciting circle of friends, and Leo loves to be loved and cherished by Taurus.

Taurus and Virgo
Love could be here to stay. You have so many good things to bring into a relationship that it would be hard to mention them all in this limited space.

Taurus and Libra
Both of these signs are ruled by Venus, planet of love, romance, art, and good living. Taurus knows all about the material side of good living and Libra knows about the romantic side—enjoy!

Taurus and Scorpio
These opposites exert a powerful influence over each other that is hard to fight, and besides, who would want to? Scorpio can bring the power and Taurus can find the money.

Taurus and Sagittarius
Interesting combination. If Sagittarius gets snared in Taurus's net, he just might want to stay there. On the other hand, Sagittarius could be the one to come to Taurus's rescue, if Taurus needs a helping hand.

Taurus and Capricorn
We call this combination "lucky in love." Capricorn could start it, but chances are that it will take a Taurus to finish it.

Taurus and Aquarius
Taurus is an earth sign and Aquarius is an air sign. Earth and air together make dust. But Aquarius can teach Taurus to fly, and Taurus can teach Aquarius how to build on a stronger foundation.

Taurus and Pisces
Friends all the way. Pisces wants to help Taurus reach their heart's desire and Taurus will show Pisces how to ask for what they really want. Ask and you will receive.

Gemini and Gemini
The name of the game is _____. The games you both can come up with stagger the imagination. Only another Gemini could keep you interested, interesting, and on your toes.

Gemini and Cancer
Slow-moving Cancer is fascinated by the swifter-moving Gemini, but the Cancer native never shows all his cards and Gemini can't stand not knowing what the big secret is. The name of this game is "Keep them guessing."

Gemini and Leo
A mutual admiration society. Leo and Gemini can make a stunning-looking couple. Leo knows all about love and Gemini can add the spice of life to the relationship.

Gemini and Virgo
In this case, Gemini and Virgo are both ruled by the planet Mercury, planet of intellect, curiosity, and mental ability. You are both full of ideas and have plenty to talk about.

Gemini and Libra
Fun and games, love and romance. This relationship is all of the above with wine, candlelight, and all the trimmings, trappings, and wrappings.

Gemini and Scorpio
There is a certain physical attraction and the sex isn't bad either, but this relationship needs lots of tender loving care.

Gemini and Sagittarius
Gemini loves being the attentive student and Sagittarius adores being the ardent teacher. You could both learn so much about yourself and life from the relationship.

Gemini and Capricorn

Capricorn can't help but catch your attention as you dash on by and he manages to keep your interest. Gemini—you love to flirt and capture Capricorn's fancy with your quick wit.

Gemini and Aquarius

Instant rapport—you are really very lucky for each other. Gemini—you are great on the local scene; and, Aquarius—you are great on a larger scale. If your partnership includes television, you could hit the jackpot.

Gemini and Pisces

Not much in common on the surface, but Pisces could be someone you look up to and respect. Pisces, on the other hand, could know what Gemini wants before they ask.

Cancer and Cancer

Kindred spirits under the skin, you could fall in love at first sight. You instantly understand each other, but a bit of warning—you could both experience a "downer" at the same time and be unable to help each other.

Cancer and Leo

Cancer adores the fabulous lion and can make money with him. Leo, on the other hand, can't understand how quickly Cancer can mirror his moods.

Cancer and Virgo

How wonderful that you found each other—how wonderful for both of you! Cancer knows how to coax a smile from Virgo, and Virgo is the friend who is always there to lend a helping hand.

Cancer and Libra

You two have admired each other from afar for a long time. Cancer has always appreciated Libra's artistic ability, and Libra has always held Cancer in the highest regard.

Cancer and Scorpio

Like a moth to a flame, you two cannot stay away from each other for long. Scorpio lights up Cancer's life and Cancer keeps the flame burning.

Cancer and Sagittarius

Sagittarius—the Cancer native is the one you can always count on to come to your aid; and you, Sagittarius, have the ability to make Cancer laugh and feel very special.

Cancer and Capricorn
This relationship has staying power. Basically you have the same goals: love, security, warmth, a home, and a family. Build on this.

Cancer and Aquarius
Cancer is about to find out that there is a big, wonderful world out there and Aquarius is ready to show it. But even if Cancer comes home early, he will "keep the home fires burning" for Aquarius.

Cancer and Pisces
Fascinating—you two appear to have a language all your own. You seem to communicate with each other without any words. Even over long distances, you manage to keep in touch.

Leo and Leo
A hard combination, because you both are leaders, but if you click it can produce one of the all-time great loves of the world that writers like to write about.

Leo and Virgo
Leo is one of the kindest people in the zodiac and knows how to appreciate all of Virgo's many talents. Virgo—you adore Leo and can overlook any flaws they might have, because you feel that they really love you.

Leo and Libra
Enjoy this relationship—you deserve to. Leo—you are the friend who can turn any cloudy day to blue skies; and, Libra—you are just the one to turn that friendship into love.

Leo and Scorpio
Sparks and fur certainly fly in this relationship. Even if you can't see eye to eye on things, the sexual attraction is incredible.

Leo and Sagittarius
If you are a gambler, then gamble on this one, because you can't help but win. You liked each other from the start and the excitement will never leave the relationship.

Leo and Capricorn
This could be a dream come true. Leo could give Capricorn the dream and Capricorn can make that dream come true.

Leo and Aquarius
What could you possibly have in common? Not much, because both of you appreciate and enjoy each other's differences.

Leo and Pisces
Leo—if you ever need a fan, Pisces is your biggest one. And, Leo—for all the love and support you get from your Pisces fan, you give just as much in return.

Virgo and Virgo
Yes, you do understand one another and can achieve a very comfortable relationship. But in a pinch, remember to be kind to one another. Most of all, be kind to yourself.

Virgo and Libra
Virgo is very creative and so is Libra. But by combining your talents you can find love. Virgo can add the fantasy, and Libra can add the romance. Together, you can create an experience.

Virgo and Scorpio
Kind of an irresistible force (Scorpio can be a regular steamroller) meeting the immovable object (Virgo can be stubborn when provoked). So something has to give, and I wonder what that is!

Virgo and Sagittarius
You can't walk in each other's shoes, so don't try. But you can and do enjoy each other's company.

Virgo and Capricorn
You work so well together, and love? Well, when it comes to love, it can, and does, last. Why? Because you both know a relationship needs to be worked at and you are both willing to put in the time it takes to make it work.

Virgo and Aquarius
Virgo could prove to be the one that Aquarius has been waiting for and Aquarius could be an innovative partner who can nurture Virgo's creative talents.

Virgo and Pisces
What could you possibly have in common? Virgos are pragmatists, with both feet always firmly planted on the ground, but Pisceans, on the other hand, are dreamers with their heads in the clouds. Now what could you two come up with if you really tried?

Libra and Libra
You are the couple voted "Most Likely to Succeed." You are the beautiful people, who are really very much in love with each other and know how to show it.

Libra and Scorpio
In a working relationship, this combination can make money, acquire possessions (of the expensive variety), and enjoy the good life.

Libra and Sagittarius
You are each known for your incredible moves. Libra made flirting an art form, and Sagittarius can come on like gangbusters. But once you get through the first rituals of courtship, you two can become very good friends.

Libra and Capricorn
Perhaps you don't appear to have a lot in common on the surface, but Capricorn, in their quiet way, can give you a material advantage, and Libra can give Capricorn the respect and class they want so much.

Libra and Aquarius
You two haven't been able to shut up since you met. You can, and will always, find lots to talk about.

Libra and Pisces
You don't seem at all interested in Pisces until they need you and then you can't help but be there. You love to be needed. Pisces—you can see that Libra is kept out of harm's way and that things always run smoothly.

Scorpio and Scorpio
Sex, passion, love, lust, power, money, fame, fortune—all of this and more could be yours, when you enter into this liaison.

Scorpio and Sagittarius
Sagittarius is just plain turned on by Scorpio and Scorpio, in turn, is fascinated by Sagittarius's philosophy of life. Don't question this one—it could be some kind of experience for both of you.

Scorpio and Capricorn
There is a meeting of the minds here. You know each other, where you came from and where you are going. Hook your star with this one and you both could be rising.

Scorpio and Aquarius
Scorpio has the power and Aquarius can introduce it to the world. The relationship's motto might be "Be careful what you ask for, you could get it." But that could be very nice too!

Scorpio and Pisces
This relationship could be a karmic one. If it is (and who's to say it isn't?), it could span time and dimension and go on forever.

Sagittarius and Sagittarius
What a fun relationship you could have! It would be a rather freewheeling one, because you respect each other's freedom, enjoy each other's company, and have so many interests in common that you can't help but get along.

Sagittarius and Capricorn
Capricorn courts the Sagittarius native in a sincere but simple, straightforward way. Sagittarius, on the other hand, finds Capricorn interesting, and Capricorn can always find money for Sagittarius to spend.

Sagittarius and Aquarius
Nice combination. You have lots of similar interests and lots to discuss. Friends first and always, with no strings attached, hold this relationship together.

Sagittarius and Pisces
Well, it will certainly be an interesting alliance! Sagittarius plays respected teacher to Pisces' mischievous student—could be fun.

Capricorn and Capricorn
You both are ambitious, intelligent, and not afraid of a lot of hard work. You do not enter into a relationship lightly, and once entered into, you make it work.

Capricorn and Aquarius
Another one of those interesting combinations. Aquarius could find Capricorn financially lucky, and Capricorn could find that Aquarius has some new, innovative ideas to make their fondest dreams come true.

Capricorn and Pisces
An immediate friendship developed here the moment you two met. No matter what the circumstances, you enjoy being together.

Aquarius and Aquarius
A pretty unusual relationship awaits you. You both have so much you want to accomplish in life that if you pool your resources, you can do twice as much.

Aquarius and Pisces

What a combination! Aquarius—you are the intellectual genius of the zodiac, and Pisces is the creative genius of the zodiac. Boy! The things you could do together!

Pisces and Pisces

A definite karmic-type relationship exists here. This could be the one that they call *déjà vu*. Perhaps you made a pact to come back together, perhaps not. If you can't make it work in this life, let it go and make it work in the next.

Appendix A

The Sun's Position During the Years A.D. 1900–2000

	1900	1901	1902	1903	1904	1905	1906	1907
Aquarius	January 20	January 21	January 21	January 21	January 21	January 21	January 21	January 21
Pisces	February 19	February 19	February 20	February 20	February 20	February 19	February 20	February 20
Aries	March 21	March 21	March 22	March 22	March 21	March 21	March 22	March 22
Taurus	April 21	April 21	April 21	April 21	April 21	April 21	April 21	April 21
Gemini	May 22	May 22	May 22	May 22	May 22	May 22	May 22	May 22
Cancer	June 22	June 22	June 22	June 23	June 22	June 22	June 22	June 23
Leo	July 23	July 24	July 24	July 24	July 23	July 24	July 24	July 24
Virgo	August 24	August 24	August 24	August 24	August 24	August 24	August 24	August 24
Libra	September 24	September 24	September 24	September 24	September 23	September 24	September 24	September 24
Scorpio	October 24	October 24	October 24	October 25	October 24	October 24	October 24	October 25
Sagittarius	November 23	November 23	November 23	November 23	November 23	November 23	November 23	November 23
Capricorn	December 22	December 23	December 23	December 23	December 22	December 23	December 23	December 23

	1908	1909	1910	1911	1912	1913	1914	1915
Aquarius	January 21	January 21	January 21	January 21	January 21	January 21	January 21	January 21
Pisces	February 20	February 19	February 20	February 20	February 20	February 19	February 19	February 20
Aries	March 21	March 21	March 22	March 22	March 21	March 21	March 21	March 22
Taurus	April 21	April 21	April 21	April 21	April 20	April 21	April 21	April 21
Gemini	May 21	May 22	May 22	May 22	May 21	May 22	May 22	May 22
Cancer	June 22	June 22	June 22	June 23	June 22	June 22	June 22	June 23
Leo	July 23	July 24	July 24	July 24	July 23	July 24	July 24	July 24
Virgo	August 24	August 24	August 24	August 24	August 24	August 24	August 24	August 24
Libra	September 23	September 24	September 24	September 24	September 23	September 24	September 24	September 24

	1908	1909	1910	1911	1912	1913	1914	1915
Scorpio	October 24	October 24	October 24	October 25	October 24	October 24	October 24	October 25
Sagittarius	November 23	November 23	November 23	November 23	November 23	November 23	November 23	November 23
Capricorn	December 22	December 22	December 23	December 23	December 22	December 22	December 23	December 23

	1916	1917	1918	1919	1920	1921	1922	1923
Aquarius	January 21	January 21	January 21	January 21	January 21	January 21	January 21	January 21
Pisces	February 20	February 19	February 19	February 20	February 20	February 19	February 19	February 20
Aries	March 21	March 21	March 21	March 22	March 21	March 21	March 21	March 22
Taurus	April 20	April 21	April 21	April 21	April 20	April 21	April 21	April 21
Gemini	May 21	May 22	May 22	May 22	May 21	May 22	May 22	May 22
Cancer	June 22	June 22	June 22	June 22	June 22	June 22	June 22	June 22
Leo	July 23	July 23	July 24	July 24	July 23	July 23	July 24	July 24
Virgo	August 24	August 24	August 24	August 24	August 23	August 24	August 24	August 24
Libra	September 23	September 24	September 24	September 24	September 23	September 24	September 24	September 24
Scorpio	October 24	October 24	October 24	October 24	October 24	October 24	October 24	October 24
Sagittarius	November 23	November 23	November 23	November 23	November 23	November 23	November 23	November 23
Capricorn	December 22	December 22	December 23	December 23	December 22	December 22	December 23	December 23

	1924	1925	1926	1927	1928	1929	1930	1931
Aquarius	January 21	January 21	January 21	January 21	January 21	January 21	January 21	January 21
Pisces	February 20	February 19	February 19	February 20	February 20	February 19	February 19	February 20
Aries	March 21	March 21	March 21	March 22	March 21	March 21	March 21	March 22
Taurus	April 20	April 21	April 21	April 21	April 20	April 21	April 21	April 21
Gemini	May 21	May 22	May 22	May 22	May 21	May 22	May 22	May 22
Cancer	June 22	June 22	June 22	June 22	June 22	June 22	June 22	June 22

1924–1931

	1924	1925	1926	1927	1928	1929	1930	1931
Leo	July 23	July 23	July 24	July 24	July 23	July 23	July 24	July 24
Virgo	August 23	August 24	August 24	August 24	August 23	August 24	August 24	August 24
Libra	September 23	September 24	September 24	September 24	September 23	September 24	September 24	September 24
Scorpio	October 24	October 24	October 24	October 24	October 24	October 24	October 24	October 24
Sagittarius	November 23	November 23	November 23	November 23	November 23	November 23	November 23	November 23
Capricorn	December 22	December 22	December 23	December 23	December 22	December 22	December 23	December 23

1932–1939

	1932	1933	1934	1935	1936	1937	1938	1939
Aquarius	January 21	January 20	January 21	January 21	January 21	January 20	January 21	January 21
Pisces	February 20	February 19	February 19	February 20	February 20	February 19	February 19	February 20
Aries	March 21	March 21	March 21	March 22	March 21	March 21	March 21	March 22
Taurus	April 20	April 21	April 21	April 21	April 20	April 21	April 21	April 21
Gemini	May 21	May 22	May 22	May 22	May 21	May 21	May 22	May 22
Cancer	June 22	June 22	June 22	June 22	June 22	June 22	June 22	June 22
Leo	July 23	July 23	July 24	July 24	July 23	July 23	July 24	July 24
Virgo	August 23	August 24	August 24	August 24	August 23	August 24	August 24	August 24
Libra	September 23	September 24	September 24	September 24	September 23	September 23	September 24	September 24
Scorpio	October 24	October 24	October 24	October 24	October 24	October 24	October 24	October 24
Sagittarius	November 23	November 23	November 23	November 23	November 22	November 23	November 23	November 23
Capricorn	December 22	December 22	December 22	December 23	December 22	December 22	December 23	December 23

1940–1947

	1940	1941	1942	1943	1944	1945	1946	1947
Aquarius	January 21	January 20	January 21	January 21	January 21	January 20	January 21	January 21
Pisces	February 20	February 19	February 19	February 20	February 20	February 19	February 19	February 19
Aries	March 21	March 21	March 21	March 22	March 21	March 21	March 21	March 21

	1940	1941	1942	1943	1944	1945	1946	1947
Taurus	April 20	April 20	April 21	April 21	April 20	April 20	April 21	April 21
Gemini	May 21	May 21	May 22	May 22	May 21	May 21	May 22	May 22
Cancer	June 22	June 22	June 22	June 22	June 22	June 22	June 22	June 22
Leo	July 23	July 23	July 24	July 24	July 23	July 23	July 23	July 24
Virgo	August 23	August 24	August 24	August 24	August 23	August 24	August 24	August 24
Libra	September 23	September 23	September 24	September 24	September 23	September 23	September 24	September 24
Scorpio	October 24	October 24	October 24	October 24	October 24	October 24	October 24	October 24
Sagittarius	November 22	November 23	November 23	November 23	November 22	November 23	November 23	November 23
Capricorn	December 22	December 22	December 22	December 23	December 22	December 22	December 22	December 23

	1948	1949	1950	1951	1952	1953	1954	1955
Aquarius	January 21	January 20	January 21	January 21	January 21	January 20	January 21	January 21
Pisces	February 20	February 19	February 19	February 19	February 20	February 19	February 19	February 19
Aries	March 21	March 21	March 21	March 21	March 21	March 21	March 21	March 21
Taurus	April 20	April 20	April 21	April 21	April 20	April 20	April 21	April 21
Gemini	May 21	May 21	May 22	May 22	May 21	May 21	May 22	May 22
Cancer	June 22	June 22	June 22	June 22	June 21	June 22	June 22	June 22
Leo	July 23	July 23	July 23	July 24	July 23	July 23	July 23	July 24
Virgo	August 23	August 23	August 24	August 24	August 23	August 23	August 24	August 24
Libra	September 23	September 23	September 24	September 24	September 23	September 23	September 24	September 24
Scorpio	October 24	October 24	October 24	October 24	October 23	October 24	October 24	October 24
Sagittarius	November 22	November 23	November 23	November 23	November 22	November 23	November 23	November 23
Capricorn	December 22	December 22	December 22	December 22	December 22	December 22	December 22	December 23

	1956	1957	1958	1959	1960	1961	1962	1963
Aquarius	January 21	January 20	January 21	January 21	January 21	January 20	January 21	January 21
Pisces	February 20	February 19	February 19	February 19	February 20	February 19	February 19	February 19
Aries	March 21	March 21	March 21	March 21	March 21	March 21	March 21	March 21
Taurus	April 20	April 20	April 21	April 21	April 20	April 20	April 21	April 21
Gemini	May 21	May 21	May 22	May 22	May 21	May 21	May 22	May 22
Cancer	June 21	June 22	June 22	June 22	June 21	June 22	June 22	June 22
Leo	July 23	July 23	July 23	July 24	July 23	July 23	July 23	July 24
Virgo	August 23	August 23	August 24	August 24	August 23	August 23	August 24	August 24
Libra	September 23	September 23	September 24	September 24	September 23	September 23	September 24	September 24
Scorpio	October 23	October 24	October 24	October 24	October 23	October 24	October 24	October 24
Sagittarius	November 22	November 23	November 23	November 23	November 22	November 23	November 23	November 23
Capricorn	December 22	December 22	December 22	December 23	December 22	December 22	December 22	December 23

	1964	1965	1966	1967	1968	1969	1970	1971
Aquarius	January 21	January 20	January 21	January 21	January 21	January 20	January 20	January 21
Pisces	February 20	February 19	February 19	February 19	February 20	February 19	February 19	February 19
Aries	March 21	March 21	March 21	March 21	March 21	March 21	March 21	March 21
Taurus	April 20	April 20	April 21	April 21	April 20	April 20	April 21	April 21
Gemini	May 21	May 21	May 22	May 22	May 21	May 21	May 21	May 22
Cancer	June 21	June 22	June 22	June 22	June 21	June 22	June 22	June 22
Leo	July 23	July 23	July 23	July 24	July 23	July 23	July 23	July 24
Virgo	August 23	August 23	August 24	August 24	August 23	August 23	August 24	August 24
Libra	September 23	September 23	September 23	September 24	September 23	September 23	September 23	September 24
Scorpio	October 23	October 24	October 24	October 24	October 23	October 24	October 24	October 24
Sagittarius	November 22	November 23	November 23	November 23	November 22	November 22	November 22	November 23
Capricorn	December 22	December 22	December 22	December 23	December 22	December 22	December 22	December 23

	1972	1973	1974	1975	1976	1977	1978	1979
Aquarius	January 21	January 20	January 20	January 21	January 21	January 20	January 20	January 21
Pisces	February 20	February 19	February 19	February 19	February 20	February 19	February 19	February 19
Aries	March 21	March 21	March 21	March 21	March 20	March 21	March 21	March 21
Taurus	April 20	April 20	April 20	April 21	April 20	April 20	April 20	April 21
Gemini	May 21	May 21	May 21	May 22	May 21	May 21	May 21	May 22
Cancer	June 21	June 22	June 22	June 22	June 21	June 22	June 22	June 22
Leo	July 23	July 23	July 23	July 23	July 23	July 23	July 23	July 23
Virgo	August 23	August 23	August 24	August 24	August 23	August 23	August 23	August 24
Libra	September 23	September 23	September 23	September 24	September 23	September 23	September 23	September 24
Scorpio	October 23	October 24	October 24	October 24	October 23	October 24	October 24	October 24
Sagittarius	November 22	November 22	November 23	November 23	November 22	November 22	November 23	November 23
Capricorn	December 22	December 22	December 22	December 22	December 22	December 22	December 22	December 22

	1980	1981	1982	1983	1984	1985	1986	1987
Aquarius	January 21	January 20	January 20	January 21	January 21	January 20	January 20	January 21
Pisces	February 20	February 19	February 19	February 19	February 19	February 19	February 19	February 19
Aries	March 20	March 21	March 21	March 21	March 20	March 21	March 21	March 21
Taurus	April 20	April 20	April 20	April 21	April 20	April 20	April 20	April 21
Gemini	May 21	May 21	May 21	May 22	May 21	May 21	May 21	May 22
Cancer	June 21	June 21	June 22	June 22	June 21	June 21	June 22	June 22
Leo	July 23	July 23	July 23	July 23	July 23	July 23	July 23	July 23
Virgo	August 23	August 23	August 23	August 24	August 23	August 23	August 23	August 24
Libra	September 23	September 23	September 23	September 24	September 23	September 23	September 23	September 24
Scorpio	October 23	October 24	October 24	October 24	October 23	October 23	October 24	October 24
Sagittarius	November 22	November 22	November 23	November 23	November 22	November 22	November 23	November 23
Capricorn	December 22	December 22	December 22	December 22	December 22	December 22	December 22	December 22

	1988	1989	1990	1991	1992	1993	1994	1995
Aquarius	January 21	January 20	January 20	January 21	January 21	January 20	January 20	January 21
Pisces	February 19	February 19	February 19	February 19	February 19	February 19	February 19	February 19
Aries	March 20	March 21	March 21	March 21	March 20	March 21	March 21	March 21
Taurus	April 20	April 20	April 20	April 21	April 20	April 20	April 20	April 21
Gemini	May 21	May 21	May 21	May 22	May 21	May 21	May 21	May 22
Cancer	June 21	June 21	June 22	June 22	June 21	June 21	June 22	June 22
Leo	July 23	July 23	July 23	July 23	July 23	July 23	July 23	July 23
Virgo	August 23	August 23	August 23	August 24	August 23	August 23	August 23	August 24
Libra	September 23	September 23	September 23	September 24	September 23	September 23	September 23	September 24
Scorpio	October 23	October 23	October 24	October 24	October 23	October 23	October 24	October 24
Sagittarius	November 22	November 22	November 23	November 23	November 22	November 22	November 23	November 23
Capricorn	December 22	December 22	December 22	December 22	December 22	December 22	December 22	December 22

	1996	1997	1998	1999	2000
Aquarius	January 21	January 20	January 20	January 21	January 21
Pisces	February 19	February 19	February 19	February 19	February 19
Aries	March 20	March 21	March 21	March 21	March 20
Taurus	April 20	April 20	April 20	April 21	April 20
Gemini	May 21	May 21	May 21	May 21	May 21
Cancer	June 21	June 21	June 22	June 22	June 21
Leo	July 23	July 23	July 23	July 23	July 23
Virgo	August 23	August 23	August 23	August 24	August 23
Libra	September 23	September 23	September 23	September 23	September 23
Scorpio	October 23	October 23	October 24	October 24	October 23
Sagittarius	November 22	November 22	November 23	November 23	November 22
Capricorn	December 22	December 22	December 22	December 22	December 22

Appendix B

Sample Cosmic Star

Aries

March 21 – April 20

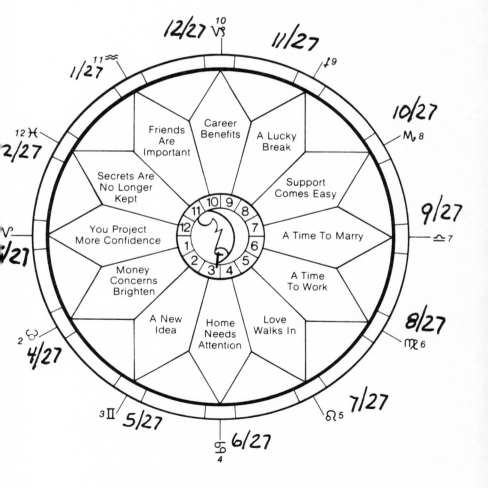

12/27 ♑ 10

11/27

1/27 ♒ 11

♐ 9

2/27 ♓ 12

10/27
♏ 8

♈
/27

9/27
♎ 7

2 ♉
4/27

8/27
♍ 6

3 ♊ 5/27

♌ 5 7/27

♋ 6/27
4

Inner wheel (houses)
11 10 9 8 7 6 5 4 3 2 1 12

Segments (clockwise from top)
- Career Benefits
- A Lucky Break
- Support Comes Easy
- A Time To Marry
- A Time To Work
- Love Walks In
- Home Needs Attention
- A New Idea
- Money Concerns Brighten
- You Project More Confidence
- Secrets Are No Longer Kept
- Friends Are Important

Bibliography

Anderson, Jennifer. *The Thinking Woman's Beauty Book*. New York: Avon, 1979.

Astarte. *Astrology Made Easy*. North Hollywood, California: Wilshire Book Company, 1977.

Cabot, Tracy. *How to Make a Man Fall in Love With You*. New York: St. Martin's Press, 1984.

Cho, Emily. *Looking Terrific*. New York: Ballantine Books, 1978.

Coffey, Barbara. *Glamour's Success Book*. New York: Simon & Schuster, 1979.

Dahl, Arlene. *Lovescopes*. New York: Bobbs-Merrill Company, Inc., 1983.

Eiseman, Leatrice. *Alive With Color*. Washington, D.C.: Acropolis Books Ltd., 1980.

Givens, David. *Love Signals*. New York: Crown Publishers, 1983.

Goodman, Linda. *Sun Signs*. New York: Bantam Books, 1968.

———. *Love Signs*. New York: Fawcett Columbine, 1978.

Hall, Manly. *Astrological Keywords*. Totawa, New Jersey: Littlefield, Adams and Company, 1975.

Hand, Robert. *Planets in Transit*. Rockport, Massachusetts: Para Research, 1976.

Jackson, Carole. *Color Me Beautiful*. Washington, D.C.: Acropolis Books Ltd., 1980.

Jackson, Gerald, and Connie Church. *Star Style*. New York: St. Martin's Press, 1984.

Kassorla, Irene. *Nice Girls Do*. New York: Playboy Paperbacks, 1982.

King, Teri. *Love, Sex and Astrology*. New York: Harper and Row Publishers, 1973.

Leek, Sybil. *The Astrological Guide to Beauty*. New York: Popular Library, 1973.

Michelsen, Neil. *The American Ephemeris for the 20th Century: 1900–2000 at Midnight*. Rockport, Massachusetts: Para Research, 1980.

Parker, Derek and Julia. *The Compleat Astrologer's Love Signs*. New York: Grosset and Dunlap Publishers, 1974.

Sakaian, Frances, and Louis Acker. *The Astrologer's Handbook*. New York: Harper and Row Publishers, 1973.

———. *Predictive Astrology*. New York: Harper and Row Publishers, 1977.

Simenour, Jacqueline, and David Carroll. *Singles—The New Americans*. New York: Simon & Schuster, 1982.

Wallach, Janet. *Working Wardrobe*. Washington, D.C.: Acropolis Books Ltd., 1981.